SNMP Application Developer's Guide

SNMP Application Developer's Guide

Robert L. Townsend

JOHN WILEY & SONS, INC.

New York   Chichester   Weinheim   Brisbane   Singapore   Toronto

This publication is designed to provide accurate and authoritative information in regard to the subject matter covered. It is sold with the understanding that the publisher is not engaged in rendering legal, accounting, or other professional services. If legal advice or other expert assistance is required, the services of a competent professional person should be sought.

Library of Congress Cataloging-in-Publication Data:

Townsend, R. L. (Robert L.)
  SNMP application developer's guide / R.L. Townsend
    p.   cm.
  Includes index.
  ISBN 0-471-28640-0
  1. Simple Network Management Protocol (Computer network protocol)
  I. Title.
  TK5105.5.T69   1995
  005.7'1—dc20   95-2739
                                                               CIP

Project Management: Jo-Ann Campbell • Production: mle design • 562 Milford Point Rd. • Milford, CT 06460 • 203•878•3793

Printed in the United States of America.

10   9   8   7   6   5

To those in my family who gave me the strength
and to those who have written a book before—
they will understand.

Contents

Introduction

When I was in my teens, my grandmother would tell me about having walked behind a wagon from Missouri to Minnesota; they didn't ride, because they wanted to keep the horses from tiring. She would tell me about the first time she saw a n automobile, and the first airplanes. Now we are in the midst of a technological revolution that is sure to bring as much change for us as the car and airplane did for my grandmother.

Technology is now overwhelming us: it is critical that we get a handle on it. We must manage technology so that it does not manage us. That implies that network management is very important. This book is dedicated to conquering the technology of network management. It will provide all the information required to understand the basics of network management using SNMP, or simple network management protocol. It will also provide significant detail relating to overall network management.

This book provides a comprehensive look at the issues surrounding network management. The focus is on SNMP, but there is much material relating to network management in general.

The material is presented so that no previous knowledge of SNMP is required. You will, however, require some background in computer networking, computer science, or some related understanding. To be able to make use of and understand the C code, the reader should be familiar with the C programming language. I have tried to take a lighthearted approach to the material, but SNMP isn't the most humorous subject in the world.

Throughout the book I have stressed the issues found in the real world. If you are looking for a protocol specification, you will find the book off base; if you are interested in developing an SNMP agent or application, you will find it very useful. Some parts of the book may be dated by the time you read it; the field changes quickly and there is some delay in the publishing process. However, I have done my best to help the practitioner rather than the theorist.

To increase the clarity of the issues, source code has been used throughout the book. A complete listing of the presented code is available on the included diskette. The book also includes a bit of background material, particularly relating to the Internet, which was the birthplace for many of the network protocols.

USING THE SOURCE CODE

About the Source Code

Included with this book is one of the most complete sets of SNMP source code available, from both the Massachusetts Institute of Technology (MIT) and Carnegie-Mellon University (CMU).

The source code was selected from a number of public domain versions. The selection criteria were portability, functionality, and appropriate comments, which were particularly important because documentation of public domain code is generally limited.

The MIT code represents an early effort. This code was called SNMP; its name was later changed to version 2, or SNMPv2. The CMU code was selected to represent SNMP version 1, since it is the basis of many of the commercial products in use today. The disk contains source for data encryption standard (DES) and serial communications as well.

The last directory on the diskette contains the requests for comments, or RFCs, that relate to SNMP, some of which are also available in a more complete form on the Internet.

Loading the Source Code

You should load the source code onto your system now, so you have access to the examples and RFCs. To load the material, simply place the disk in the appropriate drive, change your directory to that drive, and type install. Should something go wrong and the automatic installation does not work, copy the files onto your hard disk, uncompress them using—pkunzip, which is included on diskette, then untar them using the tar utility, also included.

The pkunzip command format is:

```
pkunzip <source file name>
```

The tar command format is:

```
tar-xvf <file name>
```

The source code requires a great deal of hard disk space. The install menu provides for a partial load of the source code. It may be wise to load one part at a time to assure sufficient disk space.

Internet Access

Anyone who is active in any area of computer science, especially those involved in the development of software, should have Internet access. Whether you are developing software or just hacking, the Internet is as important as any other development tool you use.

Along with public domain source code, you gain access to newsgroups and a world of information. No matter what the question, you can find some newsgroups somewhere whose members are ready to show just how much they know by answering your question. There are even newsgroups to tell you how to gain access to the Internet, on alt.internet.services.

One word of caution is in order regarding newsgroups subscription. There are hundreds of megabytes of information posted each week. You may want to subscribe to a limited number of groups until you see just how much information is downloaded; otherwise the phone line charges will be excessive unless you live in an area with local access.

If you are doing SNMP development there are three newsgroups that you will want to join as soon as you can:

- comp.protocols.snmp

- info.nysersnmp

- info.snmp

Many of the protocols related to SNMP have newsgroups also, such as the TCP/IP (transmission control protocol/internet protocol) group, SLIP (serial line over IP), and PPP (point-to-point protocol).

Some of the better known companies that provide access to the Internet are:

Performance Systems International, Inc.
PO. Box 2986
Reston, VA 22090-9862
(703) 620-6651

CompuServe
5000 Arlington Centre Boulevard
Columbus, OH 43220
(800) 848-8990

Prodigy
445 Hamilton Avenue
White Plains, NY 10601
(800) 284-5933

America Online
8619 Westwood Center Drive
Vienna, VA
(800) 227-6364

Delphi
3 Blackstone Street
Cambridge, MA
(800) 544-4005

Dialog
3460 Hillview Avenue
Palo Alto, CA
(800) 334-2564

GEnie
401 N. Washington Street
Rockville, MD 20850
(800) 638-9636

Organization

The book is organized in a manner that reflects the steps that must be taken to implement SNMP. It starts with basic information in Chapters 1 and 2 relating to how to get started. Chapter 3 lays the groundwork for SNMP development, giving you a basic understanding of network management and the protocol. Chapter 4 takes you into the supporting protocols. It provides an overview of the transport protocols and some of the issues relating to SNMP communications. Chapter 5 goes into the SNMP internals and lays the basis for Chapter 6, which deals with the management information base, or MIB. Chapter 7 provides MIB tool information and information about standard MIBs. Chapters 8 through 12 take up issues of the SNMP protocol itself. Chapter 13 describes an agent implementation based on the MIB code included on the diskettes.

As you can see, this book is not intended to provide the details of the protocol. It is intended to help get the protocol up and operational. All too often, people believe the problem is getting the protocol functional, when the real issue is the peripheral material. Most public domain agents function just fine; what you need to do is get them compiled on a target system, and correct any problems they have. But what about a MIB, what about traps, what about a protocol stack? Those are the issues addressed here. Most programmers can take the source code from the diskettes and have the agent up and operational in a week.

I hope that everyone will find this book useful and readable. Let's cut to the chase: Welcome to the world of SNMP and network management.

1

Overview

BACKGROUND

Computer networks are everywhere, in various sizes and architectures. The largest of them is the national network, commonly referred to as the Internet. It crosses the country as a highway of high speed communications circuits operating at 45 megabytes per second. The original network had thirteen hubs with primary connections to the backbone. The National Science Foundation (NSF), IBM and the University of Michigan (MERIT) founded the current Internet in the mid-80s under the name NFSNET. The NSF provided funding, IBM provided research and equipment, and Merit provided operations. Today, the NSFNET connects to many other networks, such as the NASA Science Internet, and links hundreds of universities, researchers, several super computers, and many individuals.

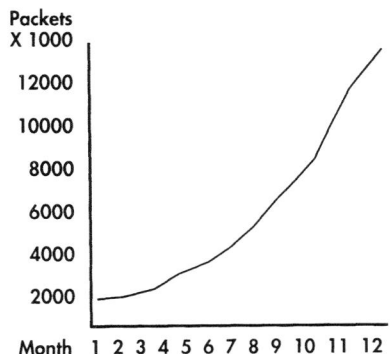

Figure 1.1. The first year traffic on the NSFNET.

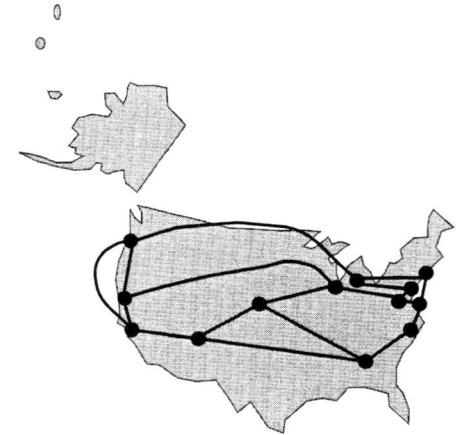

Figure 1.2. The Original NSFNET Configuration.

I had the opportunity to work with Paul Bosco, IBM and one of the original Internet promoters. Bosco consulted with me regarding performance issues; he was sure from the start that the Internet would grow so rapidly that performance would be a major issue, and his assumption proved to be correct. Within two years the network had outgrown the T1 lines (U.S. standard line speed, primarily for phone lines) and the older IBM RTs. RTs were IBM's original AIX workstations.

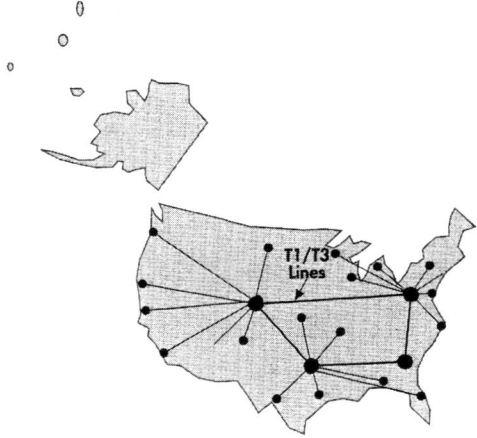

Figure 1.3 The current Internet Configuration.

When the Internet picked up the traffic from a couple of older networks, a desperate need for more bandwidth was created. I developed and deployed a number of performance enhancements that helped the network continue until the new RS6000 machines and T3 lines (U.S. standard line speed primarily for phone lines) could be deployed. The performance of the RS6000s relieved the strain at the time, but even that technology would soon be outgrown.

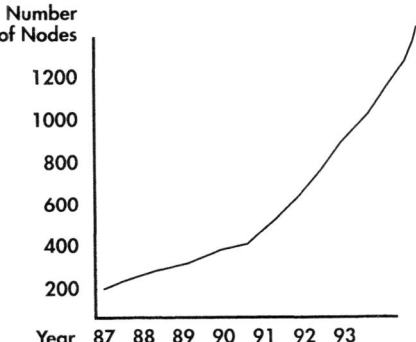

Figure 1.4 Worldwide growth.

Shortly after the cut over to T3, the planners began to work on fiber-distributed data interface (FDDI) speed equipment. Bosco believed that even FDDI would not provide all the bandwidth needed and went off to do some research with MIT on SONET (Synchronous Optical NETwork) speed equipment. I saw a need for network management and stayed on to help with that. It was then that I became involved with SNMP. It was clear that the network would need some sort of management. After all, there were sites located out in the middle of nowhere, and when something went wrong someone would have to visit the site. This was not a task that anyone wanted. Given the topology, some form of network management would help.

As I became involved with network management I also became involved with the request for comments (RFC) process and stayed with this effort for almost two years. After working on the theoretical aspects of network management, I wanted to really utilize this knowledge doing commercial implementations.

Network management became my main focus for a number of years. I worked with several proprietary network management systems as well as SNMP. I spent most of my time in the real world, working with more than a dozen clients to help them implement SNMP. It became clear that many people misunderstood SNMP, and few understood the difficulty of implementing it correctly.

SCOPE

The simple network management protocol has been well received by the industry. Virtually every vendor of network equipment must offer SNMP to be a player in the marketplace. After all, 911 emergency phone systems, cellular phone systems, and lottery systems have been using SNMP for management and control for years. SNMP is growing at a rate of 100 percent a year, and this growth rate has made knowledge of SNMP and TCP/IP necessary for every computer science professional.

SNMP is growing so quickly that it is being used over various transport protocols that do not support it as well as user datagram protocol (UDP). When SNMP was developed, only limited thought went into utilizing it with other transport protocols. SNMP was considered to be a short-term fix, while other standards were formalized. In reality it has done much the same thing that TCP has done, gained a large base that will be difficult to displace. This leads me to believe that SNMP will be with us for a long while.

Additionally, I feel that SNMPv2 will not be as forthcoming as its designers would believe. The designers may have spent too much time on theory and not enough time with the end user/implementor. The security and complexity have made it difficult to implement and there is not enough motivation to make the leap. The time spent on V2 may have actually taken some of the fire out of SNMP as a whole. Only time will tell, but if we look at OSI we might realize that if it is to complex or takes to long to implement it will lose market share. The best widget in the world isn't worth doing if it can not be sold.

Since SNMP continues to penetrate other transport protocols, there is a complete chapter dedicated to utilizing SNMP with other transport layers. It is not as extensive as it could be but it does give sufficient detail to begin an implementation with other protocols.

The first part of the book will take you through an orderly progression of SNMP, such that the reader will be able to handle any implementation of SNMP. You should come away with enough knowledge of network management to deal with most issues that come along. Yet you will not find a rehash of the protocol, you can get that from the RFCs. The book focuses on what it takes to get SNMP up and operating. The protocol has been designed by others and now it is ours to use. If what you want is to recreate the wheel and build another SNMP package you will find this lacking. If you have a package, even if it is public domain, this material will be just what you need to get it operational.

SNMP OVERVIEW

It is often thought that SNMP is a map of some network with a full color user interface. Nothing could be farther from the truth. SNMP is a protocol that runs under all of those colorful user interfaces. SNMP itself is content to operate in the background on a system and the casual observer would not realize that SNMP was even functioning. SNMP provides hand shaking between two systems. The systems will communicate information that relates to conditions of equipment or even intangibles. Intangibles being such things as general system condition, which is intangible in that you really cannot touch it. This may come from some calculation that is done on the server (agent) side of the handshaking. This information is generally requested by the client (management) side. This request comes in the form of a Protocol Data Unit (PDU). This request will traverse a network using the normal network facilities. The transport protocol and manner by which the network does its job is of no consequence to SNMP. The management station just sends out an SNMP PDU with the intent of using the information that is returned. The information that is returned may be applied to a sophisticated program that analysis the data or simply displayed on the screen for a person to evaluate. This book will deal only with the agent (server) side of the handshaking equation. The management side will be left for another day and other work. Generally the management side will consist of a product such as HP OpenView or some other management platform. Those platforms will then be expanded to cover the specifics of the network they are to be used in. Although they can provide some of the basics as soon as they are installed they cannot have the kind of intelligence needed without a great deal of software development.

Recognizing this fact, many vendors have added additional applications on top of management software. HP has added an Operations Center and is soon to announce other applications that will provide a degree of knowledge on the management station. Many vendors are adding capabilities such as "trouble ticket" generation, dispatching and other functionality that brings them closer to really managing a network.

Since the focus here is on the agent (server) side of the equation we should understand what the agent is. To better understand what it is we can look at what it is not. What it is not means what it does not do. It does not:

- function as a communications protocol

- provide a graphics interface

- inherently know about your hardware or software

- know about errors or other problems

- know about the management environment

So the next question is what does it do? Well SNMP will do a great deal but it does not have that knowledge inherently. That knowledge comes in the form of a Management Information Base (MIB). This MIB as it is called has values contained in it, much as a data base would. That is probably why it is often referred to as a database. It is actually much like a database. The dot notation used to refer to the MIB values actually provides a reference into the data. The agent will parse this dot notation, using it to get to the value that is to be returned to the management side. This value can be calculated, static or could have been updated by another application. This MIB and how it is constructed is a key element of SNMP and it will be covered in detail in this work.

A number of network products are discussed along with several new technologies. A number of the products discussed are offered on the HP OpenView platform and by a number of other vendors that remarket OpenView under their label.

FURTHER STUDY

For more information regarding topics introduced in this chapter, see *Your LAN and the Internet*, by Mark Gibbs, Network World Magazine (November 8, 1993).

REFERENCES

Fisher, Sharon. *Communications Week*, "Secure SNMP, Anyone?" April 4, 1994.

Telecommunications Magazine, Cover Story. May 1993.

An Executive Introduction to HP OpenView, Developer NSM Platform Products.

2

Vital Data

INTRODUCTION

There is a good deal of generalized information that is important to those try-ing to develop an agent or any other product relating to SNMP. This chapter covers that information. It has everything from data relating to classes, ven-dors, and more. It is a smorgasbord that should prove to be of value to every-one. It is being presented early on so you can get in touch with the people or companies needed to get the wheels turning. It will not require a detailed read-ing, but you will want to know what material it contains. Much of the material here has been gathered directly from material presented on the Internet in the SNMP news group forum.

THE DATA

The Simple Network Management Protocol is a protocol for Internet network management. Formally specified in a number of RFCs, all of the material is openly available. These RFCs are all contained on the disk that comes with this work. Many of the early RFCs are of little value and are probably not worth obtaining, while others are very useful.

Below is a break out of the more important RFCs.

- RFC 1155—Structure and Identification of Management Information for TCP/IP-based internets

- RFC 1156—Management Information Base Network Management of TCP/IP-based internets

- RFC 1157—A Simple Network Management Protocol
- RFC 1158—Management Information Base Network Management of TCP/IP based internets: MIB
- RFC 1212—Concise MIB Definitions
- RFC 1213—Management Information Base for Network Management of TCP/IP-based internets: MIB
- RFC 1215—A Convention for Defining Traps for use with the SNMP
- RFC 1442—Structure of Management Information for Version 2 of SNMP
- RFC 1444—Conformance Statements for Version 2 of SNMP
- RFC 1445—Administrative Model for Version 2 of SNMP
- RFC 1446—Security Protocols for Version 2 of SNMP
- RFC 1447—Party MIB for Version 2 of SNMP
- RFC 1448—Protocol Operations for Version 2 of SNMP

WHERE TO FIND MATERIAL

As mentioned, there are a number of RFCs contained on the diskettes, but you may find that there is other material that is not available. You can get any or all RFCs in a number of different ways. You can get them from the Internet, CD-ROM, and via Hard Copy.

You can get access to the Internet via a number of providers. A number of them are presented in the table below. The list is not complete, nor does inclusion of a provider make a statement of the quality of that provider.

Network	Service Area	
ANS	U.S. and International	(800) 456-8267
CERFNet	Northern CA	(415) 723-7520
CICnet	Midwest	(313) 998-6102
INet	Indiana	(812) 855-4240
JVNCNet	U.S.	(800)35TIGER
MIDnet	MID U.S.	(402) 472-5032
MSEN	Michigan	(313) 554-8649
NevadaNet	Nevada	(702) 784-6133
NovX	North West	(206) 447-0800
NYSERnet	NY, NY	(212) 443-4120
PREPnet	Pennsylvania	(412) 268-7870
PSCNET	Eastern U.S.	(412) 268-4960
PSInet	U.S.	(800) 82PSI82
SDSCnet	San Diego	(619) 534-5043
SURAnet	South West	(301) 982-4600
THEnet	Texas	(512) 471-3241
UUNET/Alternet	U.S.	(800) 4UUNET3
WiscNet	Wisconsin	(608) 262-8874
WVNET	Pacific	(206) 262-8874

Table 2.1 Network Access

Through the Internet

RFCs can be obtained from a service provided by RFC-INFO@ISI.EDU. You can use this service in several ways. You can ask for a list of RFCs or request them by RFC number. The lists can be searched by key such as author's name, title, date, etc. To use the service you must log into RFC-INFO@ISI.EDU with your requests in the body of the message. The request is not case sensitive.

To start you may want to request the manual. That is done by using the request:

```
help:manual
```

If you use the Internet to gather the RFCs you are cautioned to check everything along the way. Many things change daily on the Internet, and by the time this work makes it to print, the material may be dated.

You can also get RFCs at various sites through out the United States by logging in as:

```
name = anonymous
password = guest
```

Some of the locations that contain RFCs are:

- ftp.internic.net

- ftp.uu.net

- merit.edu

- nis.nsf.net

- src.doc.ic.ac.uk

- animal-farm.nevada.edu

- cs.columbia.edu

- world.std.com

A word of caution is due here. If you download all the RFCs, and you are being billed for the network time, you may want to consider what RFCs are important to you. If you download them all, make sure your bank will give you the loan you will need to pay for the service.

If you use any of these sites you can use remote printing sites as well. These sites can be used for any remote printing but we present them in the context of requesting RFCs.

Country	Code	Area Code	Location
U.S.	+1	408, 415, 510	Bay Area
U.S.	+1	317	Michigan
U.S.	+1	313	U of Mich.
U.S.	+1	301	So. Maryland
U.S.	+1	212	Staten Is.
U.S.	+1	202	Washington, DC
Netherlands	+31		Amsterdam
U.S.	+1	617	O'Reill & Assoc
U.S.	+1	718	Queens, Bronx
U.S.	+1	818	Riverside, CA
U.S.	+1	909	Chino, CA
U.S.	+1	917	NY, NY
Australia	+61		Melbourne

Table 2.2 Remote Printer Sites.

The table depicts only the area that has remote printer sites. You can find these sites in your area, through the phone directory, listed under printers.

Hardcopy

There are a number of sites from which hardcopy can be obtained, they are:

- DDN Network Information Center
  Government Systems, Inc.
  14200 Park Meadow Drive, Suite 200
  Chantilly, VA   22021
  Ph. (703) 802-4535; Fax (703) 802-8376

- SRI International
  Network Information Systems Center
  333 Ravenwood Avenue, Room EJ291
  Menlo Park, CA 94025
  Ph. (415) 859-6387; Fax (415) 859-6028
  E-mail: nisc@nisc.sri.com
  2.3.3 Via CD-Rom

You can get a CD Rom with all the RFCs from:

- Info Magic
  P.O. Box 708
  Rock Hill, NJ 08553-0708
  Ph. (800) 800-6613
  Ph. (609) 683-5501
  Various titles and pricing

- Walnut Creek CDROM
  1547 Palos Verdes Mall, Suite 260
  Walnut Creek, CA 94596
  Ph. (800) 786-9907
  Ph. (510) 947-5996
  Various titles and pricing

- In Europe, contact:
  CDROM Versand
  Helga Seyb
  Fuchsweg 86
  Tel: +49-8106-302210

ADDITIONAL INFORMATION

With the growing popularity of the Internet, the ways to access information have grown at the same rate. The type of information you want access to can also dictate the way it is accessed. For example, if there is a mailing list for the information you want, you need only subscribe; the systems will do the rest. Some of the mailing lists that are important to the SNMP community are presented below. It is a great way to keep up with what is going on. No matter how shy you may be, you need only read; no response or comment is required. It will only take a short period of time before you know the names of all the regulars. You may even wonder if some of the people do any work or just read and send mail.

Mailing Lists

- SNMP mailing list—SNMP@psi.net
  A discussion of the current hot topics in the SNMP community.

- ISO mailing list—iso@nic.ddn.mil
  Discussion of ISO standards, in some cases related to SNMP.

Each mailing list has its own benefit. There are other mailing lists relating to protocols and general discussions that may be of value as well. They can be found and checked out by cruising the Internet with any of the various packages available.

User Groups

- ISO news group—comp.protocols.iso
  Relating to ISO standards, in some cases relative to SNMP

- SNMP news group—comp.protocols.snmp
  Relating to SNMP
  SRI International
  Network Information Systems Center
  333 Ravenwood Avenue, Rm EJ291
  Menlo Park, CA 94025
  Ph. (415) 859-6387
  Fax (415) 859-6028
  E-mail nisc@nisc.sri.com [2]

BOOKS AND RELATED WRITING

There are a number of good works and each offers something different. Some are reworks of the protocol; others offer insight that is only available from those who have been in the trenches. I have added some commentary that is relevant to each work.

- *The Simple Book: An Introduction to Management of TCP/IP-based Internets*
  by: Marshall T. Rose
  ISBN 0-13-812611-9
  © 1991 Prentice-Hall, Inc.

This book was one of the first SNMP works and still serves as a primary reference for many people. It has a good deal of insight into the protocol.

- *The Simple Book: (Second Edition)*
  by: Marshall T. Rose
  ISBN 0-13-177254-6
  © 1994 Prentice-Hall, Inc.

This is the second edition of this work. It takes into account the changes that have taken place but it still focuses on the protocol and that may be what you are looking for. If you are using someone else's agent, you may not want so much of the protocol and more of how it works.

- *SNMP, SNMP V2 and CMIP:*
  The Practical Guide to Network Management Standards
  by: William Stallings
  ISBN 0-201-63331-0
  © 1993 Addison-Wesley Publishing Co, Inc.

A second printing of *SNMP, SNMPv2, and CMIP: The Practical Guide to Network Management* (Addison-Wesley, 1993) is now in bookstores. For anyone with a first printing, an errata sheet is available via anonymous ftp in the file SNMP.errata in directory ftp/pub on aw.com.

This work has a good deal of information in all areas. It tends to cover just about everything you could want as far as the protocol and the world of SNMP. Initially it received some unfair criticism. In some chapters you can tell what the issues of the moment were by the writing.

NOTE: Everyone should understand that books take months to get in print and can easily appear somewhat behind in a field that changes as fast as this. (I suppose it could be that I am just getting slow in my old age and the information is not really coming that fast. Where did I leave that crutch?)

- *Network Management: A Practical Perspective*
  by: Allan Leinwand and Karen Fang
  ISBN 0-201-52771-5
  © 1993 Addison-Wesley Publishing Co, Inc.

This is more directed at network management in general than SNMP specifically.

- *Internetworking with TCP/IP (3 Volumes)*
  Volume 1: Principles, Protocols, and Architecture
  by: Douglas E. Comer
  ISBN 0-13-468505-9 (Note: 2nd Edition)
  © 1991 Prentice-Hall, Inc.

This work has a good deal of information related to TCP/IP with chapters 25, 26 and 27 devoted to SNMP. This is early SNMP yet still very good background information.

- *Volume 2: Design, Implementation, and Internals*
  by: Douglas E. Comer and David Stevens
  ISBN 0-13-472242-6
  © 1992 Prentice-Hall, Inc.

This work has a lot of TCP/IP information with chapters 18, 19 and 20 relating to SNMP. It provides a good deal of code for study and some excellent concepts. The whole book starts to take on the feel of object-oriented coding and design that is beneficial when dealing with ASN.1 and many of the OO (Object Oriented) languages.

- *Volume 3: Client-Server Programming and Applications*
  by: Douglas E. Comer and David Stevens
  ISBN 0-13-474222-2 (Note: BSD Socket Version)
  © 1993 Prentice-Hall, Inc

This book is included primarily for its completeness.

- *Open Systems Networking: OSI & TCP/IP*
  by: David Piscitello and A. L. Chapin
  ISBN 0-201-56334-7
  © 1993 Addison-Wesley

Primarily relating to OSI, this book also contains material about TCP/IP and SNMP.

- *Managing Internetworks with SNMP*
  by: Mark A. Miller, P.E.
  ISBN 1-55851-304-3
  © 1993 M&T Books, New York, NY

The title is somewhat deceptive, since it would lead you to believe that the work was from a management perspective. It actually relates heavily to the understanding of SNMP. It is a good work for understanding the protocol through case studies.

- *Understanding SNMP MIBs*
  by David Perkins
  © 1992 David Perkins

This work is published by David Perkins and can be obtained via E-mail at dperkins@synoptics.com. It isn't clear what the cost is but it is worth what ever the cost.

- *Network Management Tools Catalog*
  by R. Stine
  NOC Tools Working Group

This work is available on the Internet at noctools@merit.edu. This work contains a number of tools that are worth knowing about. Specific to SNMP it has information related to an SNMP library and an SNMP Trap Deamon. Many of the products listed are commercial products.

- *There's Gold in them thar Networks!*
  by J. Martin
  Ohio State University
  RFC 1402

A good deal of information related to the Internet. How to get source code, books, etc.

- *A Laymans Guide to a Subset of ASN.1, BER and DER*
  by Burton Kaliski Jr.
  RSA Data Security, Inc.
  Redwood, CA

A good deal of information relating to encoding and decoding rules.

TRAINING, SEMINARS, AND MORE...

This is not intended to be an extensive list. It is merely a selective list of companies that will be around by the time this work gets out. The companies listed here have a long history of quality and reliability.

- Interop Company
  480 San Antonio Road
  Mountain View, CA 94040
  Ph. (415) 962-2522
  Fax (415) 966-5010
  E-Mail: onsite@interop.com

- Network World Technical Seminars
  Ph. (800) 643-4668 (direct: 508-820-7493)
  Fax (800) 756-9430
  [Fax back line, ask for document 55]

- Technology Conversion, Inc.
  3326 Transit Avenue
  Sioux City, IA 51106
  Ph. (712) 276-4024

One of the newest commercial products for the Internet is a product called Mosaic. It has been around in a number of forms for some time and is now commercially available from:

- Mosaic Communications Corp.
  650 Castro St. #500
  Mountain View, CA 94041
  Ph. (415) 254-1900

This is one of the best ways to navigate the Internet when looking for information.

PERIODICALS ORIENTED TO SNMP AND NETWORKING

There are more periodicals for the computer industry than any other. A complete list is outside the scope of this book, but I have listed some that seem to be more relevant than the rest.

- One bi-monthly newsletter is "SIMPLE TIMES"
  You can subscribe via email at st-subscriptions@simple-times.org
  ConneXions, The Interoperability Report
  480 San Antonio Road, Suite 100
  Mountain View, CA 94040
  Ph. (415) 941-3399
  Fax (415) 949-1779

- IBM Internet Journal
  12225 Greenville Ave., Suite 700
  Dallas, Texas 75243
  Ph. (214) 669-9000

- Network World
  161 Worcester Rd.
  Framingham, MA 01701
  Ph. (508) 820-3467

- Network Computing
  600 Community Drive
  Manhasset, NY 11030
  Ph. (708) 647-6834

STANDARDS ORGANIZATIONS

- ISO Standards
  1, Rue de varembe
  CH-1211
  Geneva 20
  Switzerland
  41 22 749-0111

- National Institute of Standards and Technology
  Rm B-64
  Technology Building 225
  Gaithersburg, MD 20899
  Ph. (301) 975-2816

- DDN Network Information Center
  Government Systems, Inc.
  14200 Park Meadow Drive, Suite 200
  Chantilly, VA 22021
  Ph. (703) 802-4535; Fax (703) 802-8376

- ISO and ANSI Standards
  American National Standards Institute
  11 West 42nd. Street; 13th floor
  New York, NY 10036
  Ph. (212) 642-4900

SNMP AGENT VENDORS

- Paul Freeman and Associates
  14 Pleasant Street; PO BOX 2067
  Westford, MA 01886-5067
  pwilson@world.std.com

- Performance Systems International, Inc.
  11800 Sunrise Valley Drive; Suite 1100
  Reston, VA 22091
  Ph. (703) 620-6651

- SNMP Research, Inc.
  3001 Kimberlin Heights Rd.
  Knoxville, TN 37920
  Ph. (615) 573-1434

- Epilogue Technology Corp.
  P.O. Box 217
  Capitola, CA 95010-0217
  Ph. (408) 426-8786

- Hewlett-Packard
  Network & System Management Division
  3404 East Harmony Road
  Fort Collins, CO 80525
  Ph. (303) 229-3800

- Technology Conversion, Inc.
  3326 Transit Avenue
  Sioux City, IA 51106
  Ph. (712) 276-4024

FOR FURTHER STUDY

The following document contains useful information that is beyond the scope of this chapter:

Krol, Ed. *The Whole Internet User's Guide and Catalog*. ISBN 1-56592-025-2. November, 1992. (Informative—relating to Internet access and usage.)

REFERENCES

Baker, Steven. *UNIX Review*, "The Evolving Internet Backbone." September, 1993.

Cikoski, Tom. *FAQ (Frequently Asked Questions)*. Newsletter on newsgroup.

3

Network Management

Network management at first glance appears to be a clear-cut issue of monitoring and control. Yet a closer look makes it clear that perspective plays an important role. Examine what network management means to the average corporation. The management perspective can be broken down to multiple perspectives, none of which would be at a low component level. The network support personnel may never relate to any perspective other than the component level, having no knowledge of the management view.

The problem becomes even worse for network equipment manufacturers. Let's consider network management from a hub manufacturer's point of view. It is easy for that vendor to see network management from the hub looking out.

All too often the communications manufacturers are driven by this one-sided perspective which is held by their technical staff. It is their perspective, but it may not be a marketable perspective. The developer must consider what the end user wants and is willing to pay a premium for. As in the computer industry, the networking area is full of better ideas that do not have a market, while the customer longs for solutions.

This book takes the perspective of its user, the SNMP developer. It does not go into the theory or the debates that surround network management. The academic types can do that.

NETWORK MANAGEMENT CONSIDERED

Network management has two main requirements, monitoring, and control. Both have various levels—physical, logical, and topology. The two requirements apply to each of the five types of management.

- Fault Management
- Accounting Management
- Configuration Management
- Performance Management
- Security Management

Network management has taken many approaches to providing network management. Some were proprietary, while others have been open protocols. Some of the protocols used include:

- HEMS—High level Entity Management
- SGMP—Simple Gateway Monitoring Protocol
- SNMP—Simple Network Management Protocol
- CMIP—Common Management Information Protocol

All of these management protocols have made an effort to manage all or a portion of a network, each gaining its own degree of success and acceptance. Each has addressed different problems of network management in different ways, some times similar and some times very different. None has gained the popular support that SNMP has. Part of that popularity is simple timing. With the expansion of the Internet and technology, SNMP was at the right place at the right time and had many of the characteristics needed. Yet it was far from an ideal solution, and there is an ever growing use of CMIP and CMIP over TCP. CMIP over TCP is often referred to as CMOT, but the CMOT RFC is outdated and the reference incorrect.

SNMP has at times received some bad press. On occasion people have been critical of its short comings, without having an alternative. No matter how SNMP is viewed, it solves some of the problems and fills a need. Whether it evolves to be the ultimate solution to network management only time will tell. Surely network management as well as SNMP will continue to evolve.

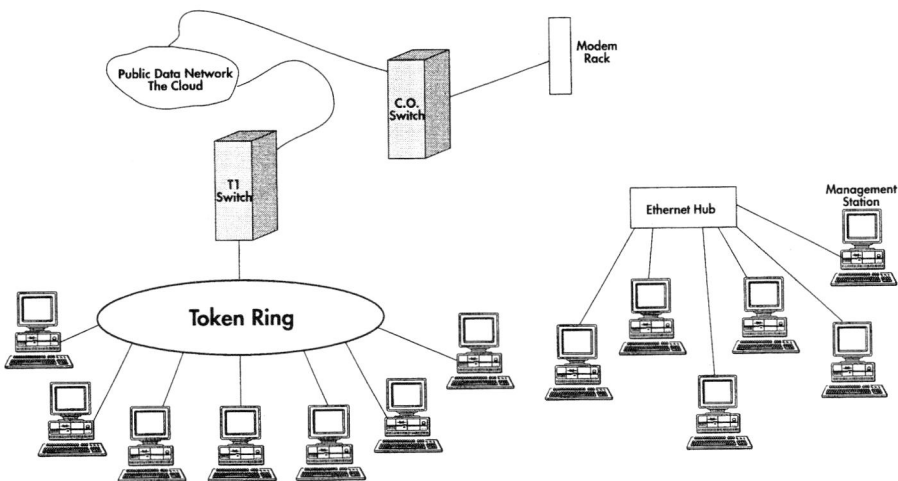

Figure 3.1 Complexity of Network Management.

Figure 3.1 shows just how complex a network can be. This growing complexity would be difficult for any network management system. SNMP was not meant to be the end. It was designed and developed to be an interim solution. Even if it had been intended to be a long-lived solution, the complexity of networks could become impossible to deal with. For example, contemplate the possibility of a network that bridged several states via leased lines and interconnected 100 sites with 2000 nodes. This is an actual implementation for which SNMP is used. The 2000 nodes are POS (Point of Sale) registers and the goal is to keep a hundred stores on-line. The network complexity exceeds anything that could be designed on a network map or even on a layered map, yet SNMP is expected to deal with such a net. SNMP actually does a reasonable job. How to represent the network graphically presents more problems. Another problem is that there are so many TRAPS (SNMP Error Notifications) at times that the network monitoring stations are overwhelmed.

As network management has evolved, there has been the perception that it is a new technology. In reality, network management has been around since the early days of computing in various forms. The early mainframes developed sophisticated networks and learned to manage them. The mainframe environments can require the management of thousands of devices. SNMP implementations, on the other hand, have trouble supporting several hundred devices. One could ask why, if we have progressed, we can not deal with the number of elements that the early mainframes could? The answer is in the complexity of the networks. The number of elements that a mainframe would manage could be quite large but they were all of a set number of types. A mainframe may manage hundreds of 3270 pieces of equipment. With limited types of equipment, using few protocols, network management is not a problem. Networks managed by SNMP may have those same 3270s talking SNA (System Network Architecture) over SDLC (Synchronous Data Link Control) through an IP network across X.25 (CCITT Standard Protocol for Transport Level) into a router on to a FDDI ring back out to a token ring back to a mainframe. This example makes it clear that the complexity of such networks far exceeds the mainframe network.

Because of this growth and expansion, many of the old ideas of network management become outdated. Protocols such as SNMP are replacing the proprietary management systems. SNMP can be used to manage complex networks thanks to the Management Information Base (MIB) concept. The MIB can be expanded to include information about all of the equipment on the network. The MIB creates the feel of an "open" architecture because the key elements of the equipment must be part of the MIB.

This requirement that the elements of the managed equipment be known to SNMP, and the MIB can, at times, create problems. As the network grows, so must the understanding and information relating to the network. The information contained in the MIB can grow very large. As the network grows, it can become very difficult to represent all of the MIB data in a reasonable manner for viewing.

Additionally the growth of information consumes more and more Network Management Station (NMS) resources. The growth comes mostly in the form of data structures used to hold MIB information. The actual data should be dynamic, since an intelligent cache scheme is impossible to build, yet the data structures are required to provide a memory location for data manipulation. In some cases this memory can be reduced through dynamic allocation, but that requires extra CPU cycles and the agent can possibly run out of memory at runtime, causing other problems.

Most of the commercial management systems address those problems in one way or another, yet no one seems to really have the answer. Companies, such as HP, have taken the approach of Distributed Management. Still others suggest layering the components of the network, while others use multiple NMSs and manage a limited number of components with each station.

SNMP Network Management

The Internet community has adopted Simple Network Management Protocol as the standard for network management. The SNMP protocol uses a query-response model, also viewed as a client/server. The client/manager end generates the queries. The server/agent generates the response. SNMP gives a management station the ability to query a piece of equipment for parameters relating to that device. The client can also generate a command to change a parameter on the agent. In addition, SNMP gives the agent the ability to notify the management station when events happen.

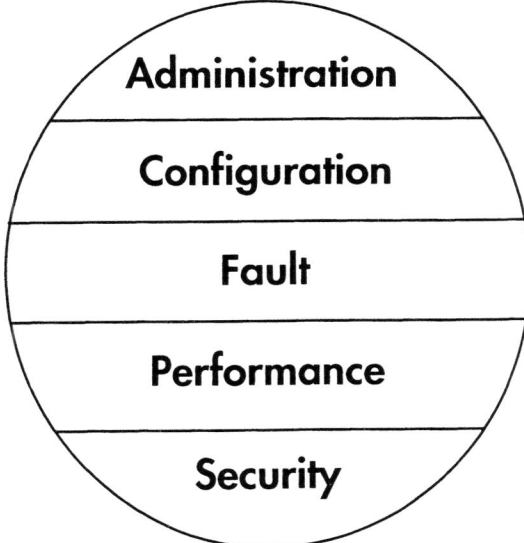

Figure 3.2 Management Functionality.

The whole SNMP environment has evolved in part with the IEEE network management mentality and in part with the OSI mentality. This combination of thinking formed a protocol that is functional while having a growth path as well as a degree of compatibility. (I am using the term compatibility very loosely in this case.)

The SNMP model and the OSI (CMIP) model do not map directly to each other. The OSI model utilizes the commands:

- get   retrieve information
- set   change values

- action   performs a command
- create   forms a new instance of the object
- delete   removes a specified object instance
- event-report   signals that an event of importance has taken place

The SNMP model uses the command set:

- get   retrieve information
- set   change values
- getnext   used to retrieve the next value in a table or row
- trap   signals that an event of importance has taken place

Some SNMP agents and managers have expanded functionality that comes close to a direct map between the two. Packages such as PEER and HP OpenView have expanded the templates to accommodate a near-direct mapping. Others have made no attempt at mapping. The industry trend is moving towards a one-to-one mapping or complete replacement of SNMP with the CMIP model. This trend is in part being driven by the telephone companies (telecos). Many have gone directly to a CMIP implementation using such products as the Redix CMIP/OSI stack. The current CMIP implementations are few and far between, but their numbers are growing every day. The problem is the same as with TCP/IP vs. the OSI Stack, the current product base. Can those using SNMP be converted to CMIP?

CMIP is gaining popularity in many circles. Such prominent vendors as HP, IBM, and AT&T offer CMIP implementations. HP and IBM both utilize the same ISO stack while AT&T utilizes the USL (UNIX Software Labs) ISO stack. The functionality available through the use of CMIP suggests that it may be utilized more and more in the future. CMIP is discussed throughout this book.

IEEE Network Management Model

Many of the works that have come from the IEEE have come under the 802 project heading. This project comes as a series of documents titled 802.X. This framework did not even begin to deal with the need for network management. Because of this the nature of network management under 802 is to provide some services at the lower layer while allocating the majority of the responsibility to the upper layers. The 802 projects were all started long before the network management issues came to the forefront.

The 802 concept of network management comes in the form of CMIP. There are a number of elements involved in this architecture, they are:

- LAN MANAGEMENT SERVICE (LMMS) which defines the services available to the user of LMMS.

- LAN MANAGEMENT PROTOCOL ENTITY (LMMPE) defines the element that is actually responsible for communicating the management information through data exchanges.

- CONVERGENCE PROTOCOL ENTITY (CPE) defines reliability and other protocol characteristics of the transport.

This provides a minimal framework for network management. It is not nearly strong enough to deal with all of the network management issues of today's vast networks. It does provide potential for the lower transport layers.

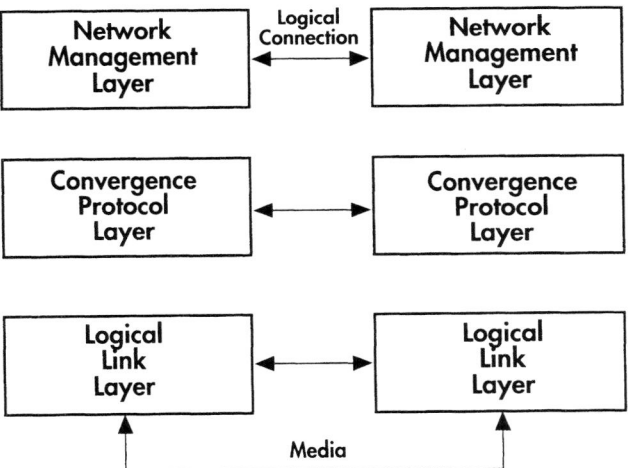

Figure 3.3 IEEE Management Architecture.

OSI Network Management Model

The OSI model, developed much later than the 802 model, provides more support for current notion of network management. It provides for network management by category. That is to say, network management is a given, and it is simply divided into categories. Those categories are:

- Fault management that defines the detection, isolation, and correction of abnormal operations.

- Accounting management that defines the ability to establish charges and identify costs.

- Configuration management that defines control of equipment and the collection of data relating to the equipment.

- Performance management that defines the performance related behaviors.

- Security management that provides for establishing and reporting security mechanisms.

These categories cover the various elements network management, but do not provide for a comprehensive approach to network management.

SNMP Network Management Model

SNMP was developed initially with thinking from both of the architectures outlined above. SNMPv2 has moved more in the direction of the OSI model. This move has also resolved some of the complaints about V1 while creating others. The evolution of SNMP will make an evolution to an OSI environment easier when and if the time came. Although many would say that SNMP is here to stay and OSIs network management will fall by the wayside, the development of SNMPv2 did help to achieve an environment that is more compatible with that of OSI. The problem is that the cost is complex, and, as could be expected, the marketplace has not accepted those changes well. To date, few vendors have chosen to implement SNMPv2. Some major organizations, such as Lawrence Livermore Labs, have chosen other alternatives that are easier.

Although it must be said that recent improvements from the user community may correct some of the over-kill of V2 Security, some of the proposals would reduce the security requirements of SNMPv2. This has been the major issue. The use of Data Encryption Standard (DES) has made V2 implementation complex, and since DES cannot be exported, it has also created a number of marketing issues. There are internationalized versions of DES available that meet all the requirements and can be exported. There is an international version on the accompanying diskettes.

MANAGEMENT VIA SNMP

SNMP uses a subset of ASN.1 (Abstract Syntax Notation) as input. The ASN input provides a method by which the data can traverse various architectures without a problem. This allows machines using an 8-bit architecture to use the same data abstraction as a 64-bit machine, or a machine that uses BIG ENDIAN architecture to utilize the same data as one using LITTLE ENDIAN.

SNMP has made networks somewhat manageable, has allowed fast implementation and deployment to become the de facto standard. Virtually every
network vendor has deployed products using SNMP. IANA (Internet Assigned
Numbers Authority) currently has over 1000 enterprise ids on file, and it grows
larger every day. The enterprise number is required for a vendor to develop a
MIB specific to their equipment. It is conceivable that a vendor could implement around the standard MIBs, although normally there are equipment
specifics that are more important for the network management. For example, a
packet in count may not be as important to a network manager as a MIB variable that reflects the percent of system utilization. A network manager may
not care about packets if the system is 100 percent busy and dropping packets
anyway. In which case the packet count may consist of retransmissions, providing a distorted count.

As the acceptance of SNMP grows, it becomes important for all computer
professionals to understand the SNMP philosophy. We need to know what the
limitations are, and what part SNMP really plays in network management.
This is as important to the developer as the code, since without that understanding it would be difficult to appreciate or do justice to an SNMP
development.

Limitations of SNMP

Probably one of the best points for SNMP is that there are few limitations. In
the creation of the SNMP protocol there was a good deal of thought given to
making it expandable. Even though the name Simple Network Management
Protocol conjures up thoughts of a limited protocol, that is not the case. The
use of the MIB approach allowed for expansion of the information base and created a protocol that could change and grow with little difficulty. The use of SMI
(Standard Management Information) to allow for MIBs that could be trans-
ported between hardware platforms made for a knowledge base that could be
utilized on most any hardware.

The MIB has also created a problem that should be understood. All too often
people will believe that SNMP, when added to a platform, is ready to go. They
give little, if any, thought to the fact that SNMP doesn't know about their
hardware. That knowledge comes from the MIB. The company implementing
the SNMP agent must develop the MIB and the code to support it. This is not a
factor for the end user, since end users reap the benefits of the vendor developing the MIB. They simply compile the MIB on their NMS, load it, and they are
ready to go. It is the vendor of the networking equipment that must develop
access routines that will fill the SNMP variable from internal equipment variables. The vendor must build the hooks to the system. For example, the vendor
may want to provide port status. They must provide a means by which SNMP

can "get" that data. SNMP receives an SNMP "GET REQUEST," parses the request to see if it is a valid MIB element, and then returns the value of that element. Returning that value may mean that some function call calculates the value or gets it in some other way but that is NOT a function of SNMP. That functionality must come from the system itself, as it interacts with SNMP.

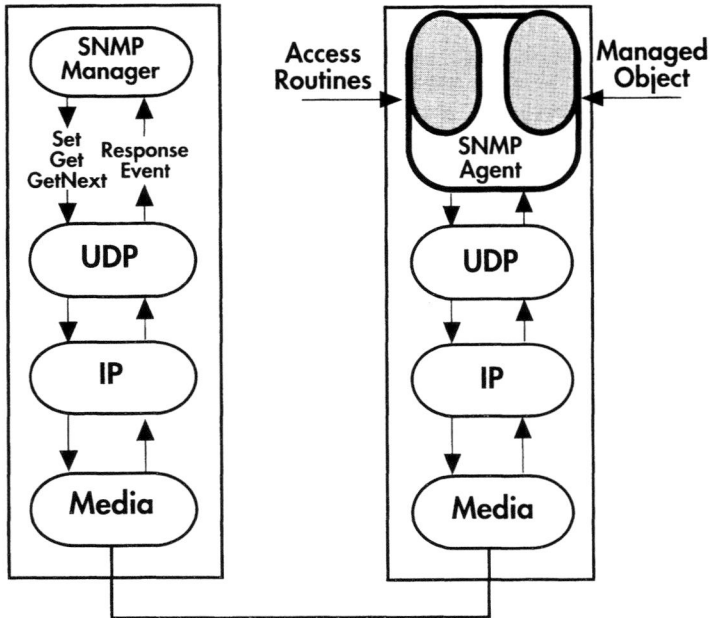

Figure 3.4 Relation of Manager and Agent.

Figure 3.4, above, shows the basic relationship of the manager and agent. All too often this relationship is not clearly understood. It is often assumed that the manager inherently knows about the equipment to be managed. Many vendors do not initially realize that they must produce SMI code (a MIB) to provide to their customer. The vendor will need to provide a MIB for every management station that is to manage the equipment. The management station must have the vendors MIB to be able to manage the equipment. The customer will compile the SMI on his or her machine, load it, and only then will the management station know about the equipment to be managed.

Often times the customer will hit some glitch when compiling the MIB, and that customer will soon be on the phone for support. This happens because all MIB compilers are not created equal. Many vendors have used one compiler to test their SMI code only to find it will not compile at the customer's site. SNMPv2 makes no difference in this area since Standard Management

Information is defined outside of the SNMP protocol. It is true that management stations, using only standard MIBs, can find many of the objects on the network but they have no management capability at that point.

Issues

Although SNMP has aged somewhat, there are still unresolved issues that need to be addressed. Some issues have to do with the overall nature of network management. The networks approach the complexity of a living organism. This complexity makes it clear that network management overall is in an embryonic state.

Another tough issue is that of applying network management across administrative boundaries. This issue is very complex and far outside the scope of this work. Suffice it to say that end-to-end management is impossible in large networks without this issue being resolved.

Still another issue is that of archival and retrieval of historic data. The current technology relates mainly to real time data. Often times a network manager needs historic data to analyze what the events were that led up to a problem. This issue requires additional work before an approach can even be developed. The issues of what data and how much data are to be archived needs consideration. An understanding of what is important data is also required. If these issues are not analyzed, there is the real possibility that storage capabilities will be quickly exhausted.

What Part Does SNMP Play?

Many end users will look at a Network Management Station (NMS) with the icons and alarms and call it SNMP. What they are actually looking at is the GUI (Graphic User Interface) front end of the SNMP protocol. It is not SNMP, and the GUI could be from any of a number of vendors. SNMP is the protocol that manages and knows about the network equipment. By having the same MIB on the management station as on the managed equipment it is able to provide lists of variables at the NMS that can be queried (get) or set on the managed equipment. SNMP will, through the use of MIB variables, allow the network manager to configure, view, and change variables on the managed equipment. In reality the network manager does little of that. The network manager will spend most of his or her time watching for alarms from the managed equipment. These alarms come to the NMS in the form of traps. The traps can cause icons to turn red or flash, and the network manager will respond to that. After receiving an alarm, the network manager may use the SNMP "GET" to retrieve variables that will help determine what has happened.

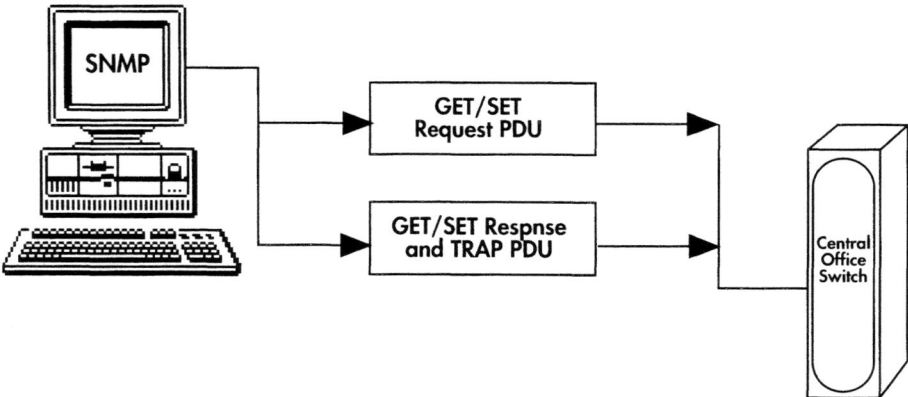

Figure 3.5 SNMP Command Exchange.

The network manager may perform any of a number of tasks using WNMP. The manager may want to balance the network load and would use SNMP to retrieve the variables that would allow him or her to determine what the through put has been. Any number of management and control type issues can be dealt with, provided the agent in the managed equipment has the required functionality. It is the conversation that takes place between the NMS and the managed equipment that is SNMP.

Much of the discussion around SNMP seems to be on the nuances of the agent workings, but I have not yet seen anyone develop an agent from square one. Most of the clients I work with start with a commercial agent or the public domain code. There are those who will say that the process should not be more complicated than this. Those who have implemented around the agent code will understand that after the agent is going, the fun is just starting. It is then that all the little routines that access values, calculate the machine uptime, and all the other variables that SNMP gets credit for are implemented. We must not forget that SNMP does not define where the data comes from, or how. Such definition is outside the scope of SNMP. Remember that SNMP is a framework that does not know about any equipment. The MIB provides that knowledge, and how all that data gets gathered. It is easy to understand that the authors could not define how to get variables on every piece of equipment and every OS ever used. Nor could they know what variables would be important on a piece of equipment, so they wisely left the how to get the variables to the vendors of the equipment.

This point is important to vendors for several reasons. First, the vendor will need to understand that every significant hardware change may require changes to the MIB. Second, the vendor must realize that if it publishes its MIB, and changes hardware, or has versions that do not support the MIB, there may be support issues that are hard to resolve. Last, but not least, is the problem of maintaining and documenting the MIB. Just to maintain the MIB for one major router vendor has required three full-time clerical personnel.

MYTHS, MAGIC, AND FOLKLORE

No writing relating to network management would be complete without a section relating to some of the myths, magic, and folklore that surrounds network management. The primary reason for such a section is to try to bring some semblance of sanity to the picture. It is common for various groups to have mistaken ideas about network management. How did they come up with such incorrect information? It is actually easy given the amount of information that flows from day to day. All too often the developers of SNMP agents have had nothing more than a few books to use for guidance, and even the best works will leave questions. Often the material will not cover the "how to" aspect of a protocol.

One myth that has gone on for some time is the idea that a PC can do all the network management. Even the Pentium chip cannot handle the load of a large network. Even if a single machine could handle the load, it would soon become I/O-bound, trying to deal with hundreds of managed pieces of equipment.

Another myth that often seems to surface is the idea that a vendor needs to support every standard MIB ever created. Vendors need to look at the cost of such thinking, as well as looking at the logic behind it. Does the material in any particular MIB have an relation to their equipment? That is to say, does a network manager really need the material from MIB II to manage the equipment, or would some other values be better?

The myths go on and on, giving the casual observer the feeling that it is all magic.

The MIB Compiler

Many development compilers will generate "STUB" function calls that can be used to help the developer. These stubs are the hooks into the system. They are the functions that are called when the SNMP agent does a "GET" or a "SET" function. These functions must be coded by the developer. The code generally requires access to variables that may only be known to the hardware developers.

These compilers will also generate the test functions used for SNMP set operations. Test functions allow the agent to "test" for the setability of a variable. These compilers generally come with commercial SNMP packages, but they cannot be found for public domain software. Many groups suggest that such compilers not be used. Many groups would rather not use a MIB compiler to help with the development effort. They feel that tighter or faster code can be achieved without using them. If a compiler is not used to generate the stub functions, the SMI encoding can only serve as a way to convey the data structures of the managed entity.

MIB compilers can relieve some of the "brute force" mentality of simply coding all of the agent interface. The tighter and faster code may be required on occasion, but for the most part, a few lines of code will not matter on a processor like the Intel 960 CA or any of the faster CPUs of today. The stubs generated by a compiler tend to help to assure that the programmer covers all of the needed stubs. The stubs also help to pinpoint errors in the SMI encoding.

Rumors

Network management can be very difficult. Much of a network manager's day is spent dealing with little issues, but when the time comes to deal with major network problems, the administrator will earn every penny of their pay. The SNMP application that a network manager is using to try to fix the problem must not be limiting. To keep the network manager from being limited, the MIB must have useful objects. A well-documented, functional, and intelligent MIB makes all the difference. The agent and MIB must provide factual data. Many agents are way off in things as simple as variable counts. Unfortunately there is a movement to simplify the MIB and agent, primarily to make the agent implementation easier. The agent and MIB should be simple in order to make the implementation manageable, but the MIB must contain enough detail for the network manager to do the job. In trying to achieve this balance some of the push for the buzz word implementations must go away. For example, the implementations that claim RMON and MIB II support may be doing more harm than good. If these MIBs have little or no relevance to the equipment to be managed, why should they be supported? For example, MIB II has no meaning at all on equipment that uses a proprietary protocol.

There has been and will be many complains about SNMPs lack of capability. It is often stated that SNMP will not provide knowledge of the status of the equipment or it won't provide usable information. There is even a debate about where the knowledge should live, on the management station, or with the agent. The management station could "GET" data and calculate a condition based upon that data, or the agent could have a variable that reflects a specific condition. Given a correctly constructed MIB, the agent can provide such information with no problem. For example, the agent could have a variable that generated an access routine that checked out several elements of the managed equipment and calculated the status of the equipment. This is not at all an unusual procedure. For example, if you study the mib2.c code you will see that the MIB compiler used, generated a function call to calculate system uptime.

```
extern int           SNMP_GET_sysUpTime();
extern void          *calc_system_uptime();
static struct attribute ATTR_sysUpTime =
{
      &ATTR_ID_sysUpTime,
      SNMP_GET_sysUpTime,
      NULL,
      NULL,
      calc_system_uptime,
      NULL,
      7,                 /* TimeTicks */
      0,
      -1,
};
```

NOTE: Throughout this work the compiler output will be that of the PEER GDMOC SMI compiler.

By viewing the code structure (above) that came from a MIB compiler, it can be understood that the SNMP agent that uses this structure makes references through pointers. It must be understood that this output will not necessarily work with any other agent code. Generally the compiler output is tuned to interface in a specific way with a specific agent. The structure indicates that it expects a function called SNMP_GET_sysUpTime to live outside this file. It expects that function to do some calculation and to return the system up time as an integer.

NOTE: In the SNMP world, system up time is a calculation reflecting how long the SNMP system has been operational, not how long the system itself has been up. This indicates that the "startup" of SNMP must save the system time in a variable to be used later to calculate SystemUpTime. The calculation would go something like:

current time - saved time = uptime

This same MIB stubs could be used to provide MIB variables that have a good deal of intelligence and meaning to the management station. For example the agent MIB could have a variable that reflects overall condition of the system. This could be a calculated value using several factors to indicate the overall system condition.

FOR FURTHER STUDY

The following documents contain useful information that is beyond the scope of this chapter.

HP OpenView Distributed Management
Communications Infrastructure Programmers Guide
Part No. J2319-90003, © July, 1992
Peer SNMP Programmers Guide
Peer Networks Inc.
3375 Scott Boulevard
Santa Clara, CA 95054 (SNMP programming information.)

HP OpenView SNMP Agent Administrator's Reference
Hewlett-Packard Company
3404 East Harmony Road
Fort Collins, CO 80525-9599
Ph. (303) 229-2321 (SNMP Agent information.)

REFERENCES

Duffy, Jim. *Network World*, "User helps vendors bring v2 to the market." January, 1994.

Fisher, Sharon. *Communications Week*, "Secure SNMP, Anyone." April 4, 1994.

Gaskin, James. *Network Computing*, "UNIX Network Management is Surely in Your Future." January 15, 1994.

Stallings, W. *STACKS: The Network Journal*, "New Life for SNMP." June, 1993.

4

SNMP Transport

INTRODUCTION

Having looked at the basics of networking and SNMP, we will now look at the protocol that carries the SNMP message. The transport protocol is not part of SNMP, but SNMP was designed with the Internet in mind and has close ties to User Datagram Protocol (UDP). SNMP can be used with any of a number of transport protocols if they provide the required support. The demands placed on the transport protocol are few, making it easy to use SNMP with various protocols. One problem that SNMP does pose for a number of transports is the connectionless mentality. For example, the trap mechanism can send a trap given a specific condition. The condition can happen at any time. This creates real problems for connection-oriented protocols, dial-up protocols, and most Wide Area Network (WAN) environments. That is not to say that it cannot be done, but it does mean that the SNMP agent should use a good deal of sanity in developing a strategy for sending TRAP Protocol Data Units (PDUs).

THE LAYERING

UDP is the transport of choice for SNMP, although it can be used with any transport that will support its requirements. Since SNMP was intended as an interim solution, other transport protocols did not get a lot of consideration. During the original design it was thought that OSI could deal with the other protocols, and SNMP need only to provide an interim solution for the Internet and a TCP/IP environment. Even with this limited scope, SNMP took the approach of layering. This layering of SNMP over UDP over IP is the norm for the Internet world. Unfortunately many do not hold to the layered module as much as one would like. Many agents can be found that embed the transport in the SNMP agent. This is often seen in PC environments. Often the PC SNMP agents will work through socket drivers that are layered over media drivers. Many will simply throw out any layering in between SNMP and the socket layer. This approach somewhat destroys the protocol stack, yet at times it is the only way to squeeze SNMP into a system. In cases such as embedded systems there often is not enough memory available to do anything else. In reality if the SNMP agent works correctly, how the layering is done becomes a moot point.

Figure 4.1 below shows how SNMP is positioned on UDP/IP stack in the normal implementation.

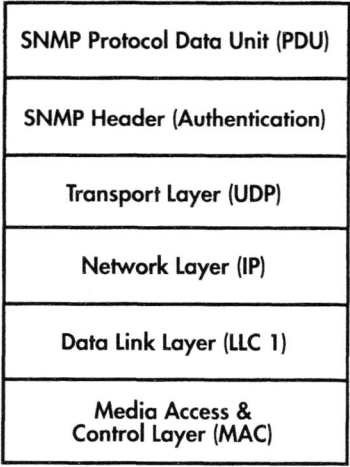

| SNMP Protocol Data Unit (PDU) |
| SNMP Header (Authentication) |
| Transport Layer (UDP) |
| Network Layer (IP) |
| Data Link Layer (LLC 1) |
| Media Access & Control Layer (MAC) |

Figure 4.1 SNMP—UDP Layering.

THE COMMON TRANSPORT

No matter which side, manager, or agent the SNMP PDU comes from, the transfer takes place in the same manner. That is, the data is formulated into an SNMP packet. After the data is placed in the buffer it is ASN.1 encoded. UDP then takes the hand off of the packet. This hand off comes only when the packet is ready to be sent. UDP gets the port number that it is to use with the packet.

NOTE: The port abstraction is an old and well-worn method of associating a structure definition with an application. The structure will contain data that allows the operating system to figure out where to send the data. It should be understood that there are two ports involved, the source and the destination. The destination port can be on the same machine as the source.

The UDP port number also provides a reference to the protocol that is the Upcall (the protocol that is above UDP) associated with this packet. The port numbers used by SNMP are "well known" ports. That means that the port numbers are set aside for the use of SNMP. The port numbers 161 and 162 are for SNMP usage. With 161 for normal SNMP exchanges and 162 for trap messages. These port numbers need to be set up somewhere for SNMP to access. In a UNIX environment the ports get set up in "/etc/services." On an embedded system, generally there will not be a file structure and the port number gets hard wired into the code.

NOTE: For SNMP implementations using SMUX the port 199 has been set aside for SMUX use.

The UDP port is mapped to a socket. The socket abstraction is also associated with a structure that is used to provide additional information to the operating system about the actual "place" to send the data.

NOTE: Place as used above may mean an interrupt vector, a memory address, or any of a number of other methods used to direct the operating system.

Many operating systems and protocol stacks are moving away from the socket abstraction to the file descriptor abstraction. That is to say, rather than opening a socket, the protocol stack would open a file descriptor that just happened to be a network device. When the protocol stack opened the file descriptor it would actually be setting up all the structures and memory required for the media adapter.

Application Layer
Presentation Layer
Session Layer
Transport Layer
Network Layer
Data Link Layer
Physical Layer

Figure 4.2 ISO Model Stack.

It must be noted that below that session layer it is acceptable for the OSI stack to utilize the IP protocol. This is a common approach in the U.S. but much less acceptable in Europe.

Services Required

SNMP places a number of requirements on the transport protocols that support it. In comparison to other applications, the requirements are few. SNMP assumes a Transport and Network protocol stack is present. Without the protocol stack, the SNMP PDU will not be sent.

NOTE: In reality the SNMP agent will not build without the transport being resolved.

The layers used by SNMP should be able to provide at least five functions. They are:

- **End-to-End Checksum**: Greatly enhances the reliability of the data transfer.

- **Multiplexing/Demultiplexing**: Provide multiplexing and demultiplexing services.

- **Routing**: Routing improves the overall utility of network management by being able to re-route packets around failed areas. This allows network management to continue operating during localized loss of service.

- **Media Independence**: This capability allows many different types of network elements to be managed. Tying SNMP to a particular data link protocol limits the ability of SNMP to manage a variety of network equipment.

- **Fragmentation and Reassembly**: This is related to media independence.

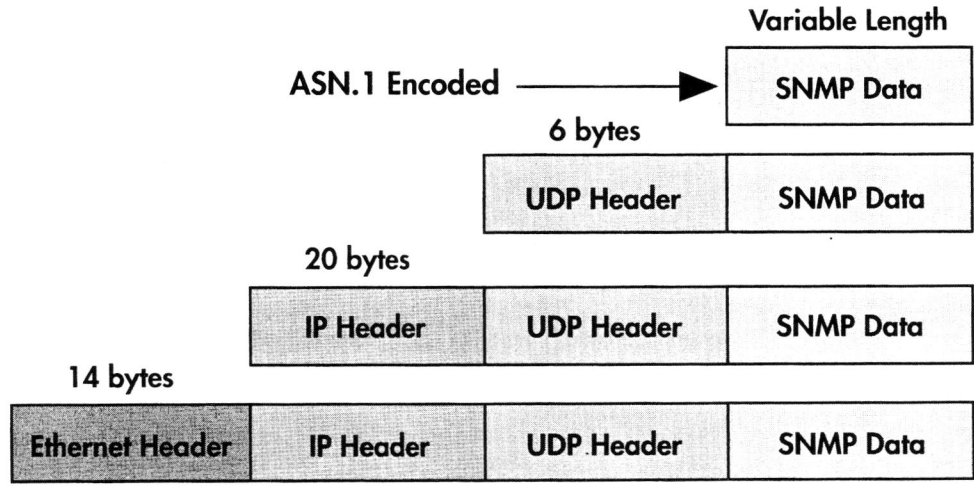

Figure 4.3 SNMP—Transport Layers.

The requirements are not absolute and they can often be worked around. For example, on a dedicated secure network such as a financial network, routing may not be required. Fragmentation and reassembly may not be required if the media does not fragment, and some protocols do not support or require checksums. The requirements are based upon the ideal environment, and they are not always essential for SNMP as for reliable communications.

NOTE: There are a number of RFCs that address SNMP utilizing transports other than SNMP, and the reader should refer to the RFCs for detail of that particular transport.

SNMP PDU (PROTOCOL DATA UNIT)

The SNMP PDU is first formulated using ASN encoding. It is then placed in a buffer, and UDP is told to "do its thing." SNMP calls the UDP service to carry the PDU using the UDP API.

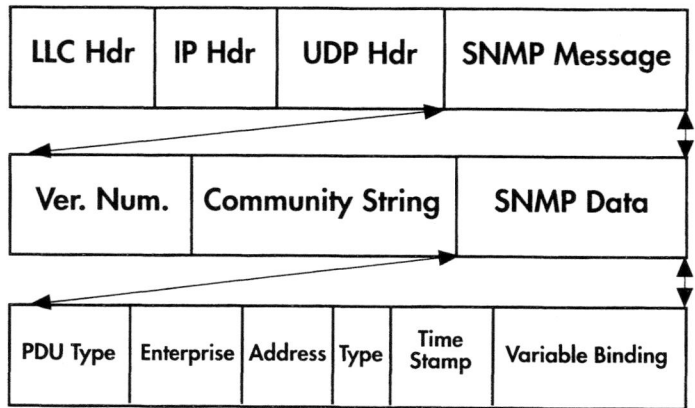

Figure 4.4 SNMP PDU.

The SNMP PDU consists of a number of fields.

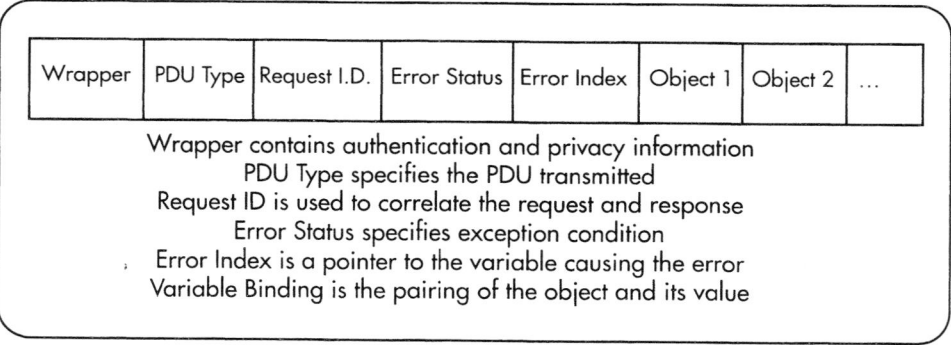

Figure 4.5 SNMP PDU with Detail.

The SNMP PDU is placed in the data area of a UDP datagram. The data area of a single UDP datagram is usually sufficient for an SNMP PDU, even when the SNMP PDU has multiple variables bound to it. (More on multiple bindings later.)

UDP DATAGRAMS

The SNMP PDU is handed off to the UDP protocol or whatever other protocol may be used for transport. UDP provides a connectionless architecture that can make using SNMP difficult at times. For example, during a series of sets, one may fall through the "cracks" and not be delivered. The network manager will not know this has happened. It would be difficult at best to generate a MIB that would be able to determine that it had received all the rules in the form of SNMP SET commands. Therefore, the manager will need to do a number of SNMP GET commands to assure that all the SETs got through given the unreliable UDP protocol. Even when a reliable transport protocol is used, it is wise to follow a SNMP SET with a GET to assure that the variable was set. It is true that there is an SNMP response generated by the agent for every message it receives, but over an unreliable protocol, you cannot be sure that the response is going to get to you. That means that the manager will need to provide a good deal of intelligence relating to how the agent should perform. Many SNMP MIBs do not provide sufficient descriptions (information) to understand the relation of one piece of data to another. Often times this aspect of the MIB data is not even considered.

NOTE: In the scenario above it was assumed that the variables were sent with separate PDUs. In some cases it is possible to use multiple variables bound to one PDU.

The Datagram

The SNMP PDU described above is encapsulated in the UDP datagram. Figure 4.6 depicts this encapsulation technique.

Source Port Filled in when UDP message arrives	Destination Port Filled in when the agent code starts
Length Filled in from size of the message	Checksum Calculated
Data Area which contains the SNMP PDU	

BITS 0 1 2 3 4 5 6 7 8 9 10 11 12 13 14 15   16 17 18 19 20 21 22 23 24 25 26 27 28 29 30 31

Figure 4.6 SNMP—UDP Datagram.

As can be seen in the drawing, the fact the UDP Datagram contains an SNMP PDU is of no real concern to UDP. It is simply going to hand off to IP without regard to what it is carrying for data. When it hands off to IP, we get one more layer of encapsulation, and we are that much closer to the data being put on the wire.

Below is an example of UDP code that utilizes the socket abstraction and therefore does not call IP directly. The calls to IP are made by the socket layer.

```
/************************************************************************
The include files assume the Berkeley UNIX environment.
************************************************************************/


#include        <sys/types.h>
#include        <sys/socket.h>
#include        <netinet/in.h>
#include        <ctypes.h>
#include        <debug.h>
#include        <local.h>
#include        <udp.h>

typedef struct UdpTag {
                    int        udpSocket;
                    struct  sockaddr       udpSockAddr;
                    CIntfType       udpRefCnt;
                    }UdpType;

typedef UdpType *UdpPtrType;
SmpStatusType udpSend (udp, bp, n)
SmpSocketType udp;
CBytePtrType bp;
CIntfType n;

{
UdpPtrType      tp;
int     result;

/************************************************************************
 * Check that there is a valid socket

************************************************************************/
if (udp == (SmpSocketType) 0)
        {
      return (errBad);
        }

tp = (UdpPtrType) udp;
/************************************************************************
```

```
 * Set up a do loop to assure that all of the data is sent.
 * Call protocol stack to send the data - function call sendto

 *************************************************************************/
        do {
                result = sendto (tp->udpSocket, (char *) bp, (int) n, (int) 0,
                        & (tp->udpSockAddr), sizeof (struct sockaddr_in));
                n -= result;
                bp += result;
                } while ((result > 0) && (n > 0));
 /*************************************************************************
 * This error can never happen theoretically but it has.

 *************************************************************************/
        if (result < 0) {
                perror ("udpSend");
                return (errBad);
                        }
        else

                        {
                        return (errOk);
                        }
}
```

THE IP PACKET

IP provides more to the transfer than another layer of code involved in the transport of the data. It provides the ability to fragment the packet and do the routing to get it to the other end. The IP interface and a short segment of code are presented below to aid the understanding.

```
/*************************************************************************
The include files assume the Berkeley UNIX environment.
*************************************************************************/
extern struct mib_ip ip_mib;
extern struct mib_icmp icmp_mib;

static int    err_cksum = 0;        /* checksum error                    */
static int    err_small = 0;        /* packets smaller than minimum      */
static int    err_header = 0;       /* packets smaller than length field */

int ip_output(mp, src_netp)
register mblk_t *mp;
NET_ENTRY *src_netp;
{
int    bcast;
int route_opt = 0;
unsigned char *optptr;
```

```
int optlen;

uph = &((S_IP_TX *)mp->b_rptr)->uph;
/*****************************************************************************
 * Validate that there is a new packet.

 *****************************************************************************/
if (!src_netp) {                      /* NEW! packet from UDP */
            uph->ps_offset = 0;
            uph->ps_pkt_type = PS_FROM_ME;
            if (uph->ps_ttl == 0)
                    uph->ps_ttl = ip_mib.ipDefaultTTL;
/*****************************************************************************
 * If SNMP stats are defined we will help to keep the stats. This is where the
 * SNMP variable is updated. The variables can be updated by the code as is
 * done here or the SNMP agent can extract the values in some way. Although
 * when it comes to counting packets and the like it is difficult at best
 * trying to do the counting outside of the transport protocol. This segment
 * supports SNMP.

 *****************************************************************************/
#ifdef SNMP_STATS
            ip_mib.ipOutRequests++;
#endif
      }

optptr = (unsigned char *)(uph->ps_options);
optlen = uph->ps_optlen;
/*****************************************************************************
 * Check to see if we are dealing with a broadcast  packet.

 *****************************************************************************/
if (bcast = is_nw_bdcst(uph->ps_dst.typec))
      {
      if (!gwy_lookup(uph->ps_dst.typec, &first_hop, -1) ||
            first_hop == BDCST_PKT)
            {
            for (snp=net_entry; snp < NetNum; snp++)
                  {
```

As can be seen from the IP code segment, SNMP variables get updated in the code. You will need to add such counters to your IP, UDP, and ICMP code to support the various MIB variables should you use those MIB groups. Your existing IP code may already support such counters. However, some protocol stacks do not provide SNMP support in the IP code. When SNMP is not supported by the protocol, it can be simulated elsewhere, but it is never as accurate as when it is done in the transport layer. In some cases the vendor of the transport will provide a stack that does support SNMP. In other cases, the vendor will not support SNMP, and you cannot get the source. In those cases the only alternative is to simulate the counters as accurately as possible.

Version	IHL	Type of Service	Total Length	
Identifier			Flags	Fragment Offset
Time to Live		Protocol	Header Checksum	
Source Address				
Destination Address				
Options and Padding				

Figure 4.7 IP Header.

The UDP code would need to call the function "ip_output(mp, src_netp)" to send the packet. You will note that in the code itself there is reference to UDP showing clearly the interrelationship of UDP and IP.

SNMP INPUT

The segments above deal with the out bound packets. This section describes the steps taken to receive a packet. For the most part it is the reverse of the packet send.

It is important to understand that when the packet is received, the first step is for IP to strip off the IP header. IP will check the validity of the packet and then hand off to UDP if UDP is the protocol referenced in the header data. In the case of SNMP, the upper protocol will probably be UDP. UDP will strip off the UDP header after validating the packet.

NOTE: Both IP and UDP are clearly defined in RFCs, and a very simple view is being presented here. It should also be understood that a media header would actually precede the IP header. The media header may be token ring, ethernet, or any of a number of other media types.

UDP will note the "PORT" identifier and associate that port with SNMP. Recall that the SNMP port number is 161, and no other protocol is to use that number. UDP then knows that it is to schedule an interrupt and call SNMP. If someone sends garbage to your IP address with the SNMP port set in the UDP header, that garbage could get to the SNMP agent. Many agents have some routine that attempts to recover a bad PDU. If the packet is completely garbage it gets discarded. Many garbled PDUs can be recovered to some degree. In the case of a PDU with multiple variables bound to it the error status becomes important because of the all or none approach to variable bindings used in SNMPv1.

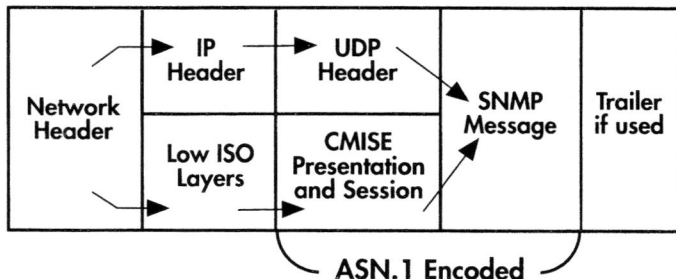

Figure 4.8 SNMP Message.

TLV (TYPE, LENGTH, VALUE)

The external representation of SNMP data is much different from the internal representation. External meaning when the PDU is outside of the hardware on the wire. Externally an SNMP PDU is represented as TLV (Type, Length, Value). The three fields break out as follows:

Figure 4.9 TLV Format.

Type Field Encoding

Look at the TLV Format in Figure 4.9. Note that the Type Field is the first field. The type field can be any of the fields represented in Tables 4.1-4.3. Each of the types, known as a TAG, is represented as a HEX value. The TAG is used in various ways in different agents. Some agents will take advantage of the TAG field information while others will make less use of the implications of the field. The agent can make a fast determination relating to the PDU based on the TAG.

UNIVERSAL CLASS	Type Field Value
INTEGER	00000010 = 02H
OCTET STRING	00000100 = 04H
NULL	00000101 = 05H
OBJECT IDENTIFIER	00000110 = 06H
SEQUENCE	00110000 = 30H
SEQUENCE OF	00110000 = 30H

Table 4.1 Universal Class.

APPLICATION CLASS	Type Field Value
IpAddress	01000000 = 40H
Counter	01000001 = 41H
Gauge	01000010 = 42H
TimeTicks	01000011 = 43H
Opaque	01000100 = 44H

Table 4.2 Application Class.

CONTEXT-SPECIFIC CLASS	Type Filed Value
GetRequest	10100000 = A0H
GetNextRequest	10100001 = A1H
GetResponse	10100010 = A2H
SetRequest	10100011 = A3H
TRAP	10100100 = A4H

Table 4.3 Context-Specific Class.

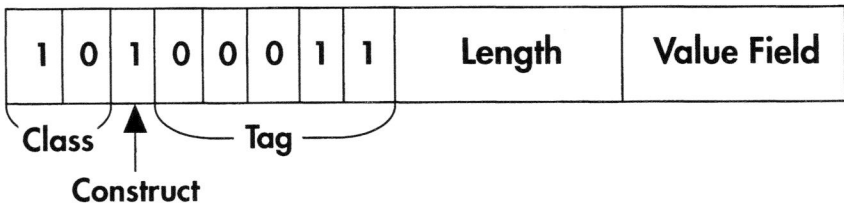

Figure 4.10 Type Field Encoding.

The agent can make determinations of the validity of the entire PDU using the type field.

Length Field Encoding

The length field contains, in octets, the length of the contents in one of three forms. The forms are:

- definite short (0)
- definite long (128)
- indefinite

SNMP prohibits the use of indefinite.

Bits	8	7	6	5	4	3	2	1
Number of Octets in Value Field	0	1	2	3	4	5	6	7

Short Definition Form - Length = 0 - 127 Octets

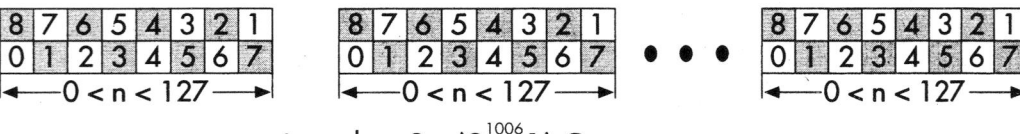

Length = $0 - (2^{1006}-1)$ Octets
Long Definition Form

Figure 4.11 Length Field Encoding.

The encoding being described relates to the ASN encoding. This encoding and decoding is provided by a BEDL (Basic Encoding and Decoding Library). The purpose of encoding and decoding is to allow communications between architecturally different systems. Consider the case where a management station using a 32-bit Big Endian architecture wanted to communicate with an 8-bit Little Endian architecture. There would need to be a conversion on the sender side and then again on the receiver side. Such conversions can eat up CPU time as well as being difficult to code. By using ASN encoding we remove such problems. By studying the debug output in the appendix the reader can see the lengthy steps that the BEDL goes through to encode or decode the data.

Value Field Encoding

The value field contains zero or more octets and conveys the value of the data. Each octet contains a digit or character of information. Should it be that the value is a term like "foo" it would be represented in the value field as three octets (see Figure 4.12).

Type Field	Length Field	Value Octet #1	Value Octet #2	Value Octet #3

Figure 4.12 Value Field Encoding.

The PRIMITIVE types that can be contained in this field are:

- NULL
- INTEGER
- OCTET STRING
- OBJECT IDENTIFIER

The UNIVERSAL aggregate types (specific to SNMP) are:

- SEQUENCE
- SEQUENCE OF

The NULL primitive shall not contain any octets, and the length octet must be set to zero. The INTEGER value must be a primitive consisting of one or more octets. The smallest number of octets possible shall be used. The OCTET STRING, UNIVERSAL type 4, contains from zero to many octets related to the data value. The OBJECT IDENTIFIER contains octets of an ordered list of sub-identifiers concatenated together. Each sub-identifier is represented by one or more octets. If the sub-identifier is 128, it is split into a series of 7-bit pieces, each in its own octet. The last of the series is identified by the MSB (most significant bit). Zero representing the last octet, while all other octets contain a one. The first octet must not equal 80H, since that is used to compress out leading zeros.

This may seem to be of little significance to the implementor and of more use to an SNMP developer. In fact, this is relatively important. In cases where the SNMP application is in question you may find it useful to look at the data going over the wire. A network analyzer would present the data such that you would need to understand how the octets should be laid out. It is just as important when dealing with the agent itself, since many agents will display the octets for debug purposes.

CMIP

Several of the major SNMP Management Software vendors base their products on the HP OpenView software. IBM, DEC and AT&T/NCR all utilize the HP code to develop their management station software. Thus, it is likely they all have some elements in common. One thing that they all have in common is that they offer an OSI/CMISE stack. The native stack offered by HP OpenView is based upon the ISODE (International Standards Organization Decode/Encode) releases. The interface complies with ROSE (Remote Operations Service Element) standard. This layers over the LPP (Lightweight Presentation Protocol) which is layered over UDP/IP. The CMISE (Common Management Information Services Element) complies with ISO DIS 9595/9596 standard. This layering complies with the ISO standard and delivers the CMOT implementation. Several of the vendors using the OpenView code have replaced these layers with their own stack. One of those vendors, AT&T, utilized the UNIX Software Labs (USL) ISO stack.

There are several good works relating to the ISO stack, and they should be consulted for a better understanding of the ISO stack. It is also helpful to review the ISODE code available on the accompanying diskettes.

The ISO stack can be taken to mean many layers. All of the upper layers of the ISO stack use BEDL's to encode and decode packets above and beyond the data encoding and decoding. When the upper layers of the ISO stack are used with UDP/IP it is commonly referred to as CMIP over TCP/IP.

The upper layers provide all of the Presentation Layer primitives and are interfaced to the lower layers through some abstraction. In System V the abstraction is the TLI (Transport Layer Interface) while in other operating systems the file abstraction is used.

FOR FURTHER STUDY

The following documents contain useful information that is beyond the scope of this chapter.

Comer, Douglas E. *Internetworking with TCP/IP (3 Volumes)*. Prentice-Hall, Inc. 1991. (All three volumes have much to offer.)

Henshall, John and Sandy Shaw. *OSI Explained.* Ellis Horwood Publishing. (Good introduction to OSI.)

OVWindows and SNMP Platform, Hewlett-Packard, 3404 East Harmony Road Fort Collins, CO 80525-9599. (General SNMP information HP University)

REFERENCES

Comer, Douglas E. *Internetworking with TCP/IP* (3 Volumes). Prentice-Hall, Inc. 1991.

5

SNMP Internals

INTRODUCTION

Every agent ever written has some differing approach to handling the internal workings of the agent. The code and how it works, provided it works, is not as important as the Application Programming Interface (API). Some of the agents have chosen to publish this interface. One that has published its interface comes from Paul Freeman and Associates. The document is included on the accompanying disk. More vendors should publish their interface, or adhere to a currently published one, thereby creating some type of standard. Publishing the interface makes the utilization of the agent much easier. Unfortunately in a world of trade secrets and proprietary information, this is not likely to happen.

Many of the currently available agents are targeted at UNIX, or MS-DOS. Because of this, there is often an issue with the porting of the agent to an embedded system. Many embedded systems run on a real time OS such as PSOS or VRTX. These operating systems have their own compilers as well as a specific way of processing. There must be more agents developed for real time environments or agents that are more portable. The problem is made even worse when a MIB compiler is used. The MIB compilers generally utilize the host compiler to compile the MIB. The MIB compiler will run in several passes. The first pass handles the Standard Management Information (SMI) code, converting it to code acceptable to a "C" compiler. This first pass is generally done utilizing the host compiler. Even though the executable that runs may be called something entirely different it is actually utilizing the host compiler. On a UNIX system the process will fork and exec the "cc" compiler. The developer must be sure that, in the case of a cross compile the correct compiler is used.

Often times this will not be the same compiler found in /usr/bin. The MIB compiler then runs the "C" compiler and leaves the output of the token pass (first pass). This leaves "C" code that can be compiled at a later time when combined with the agent code.

Regardless of the agent's nature, target environment, or logic, there are a number of constants that all agents must adhere to. It is those constants that we will address here. The method of coding or logic that could be used is beyond the scope of this book.

THE MIB

A number of SNMP agents are available, both commercially and as public domain. Some of the commercial agents carry price tags in the thousands of dollars. That price includes source code that you compile on your platform. No matter how you get your agent—commercial or public domain—a large portion of the work is in creating the MIB and its data relations.

Many will say that doing the agent code is the majority of the work. There may in fact be a good deal of work there, even if you start with a commercial agent, but the MIB and its support logic will prove to take the most time. No agent can possibly know about the hardware unless someone has done a MIB for that exact platform and is willing to provide it. This is one of the most misunderstood areas for SNMP implementations, since many believe that all the user needs to do is get the agent on the hardware and SNMP is ready to go, not so.

There is much hoopla about MIB II and the other MIBs that are currently defined, but I have found very few clients who can gain complete benefit from the standard MIBs unless they are building a router or bridge. There are a number of MIBs for the standard technologies, but in many cases they have taken the approach of trying to cover every possible variable that could exist for the protocol or platform. An approach that would make things a bit easier would be to define the very minimal basics and let each vendor expand with the specifics of its equipment. A company doing a proprietary piece of equipment probably will not care if it can provide the user with the number of packets dropped. In some cases it is in the vendors best interests if the number of packets dropped is not known. For that matter the equipment may not even keep such a count and may have to do a great deal of work to provide such a count.

There is an RFC that covers MIB II so it will not be presented here. Instead we focus on the creation of an MIB that relates to the proprietary equipment and protocols.

Hundreds of issues can arise in the creation of an MIB. In all cases, the creation of the MIB must start with data gathering. Data gathering relates to determining what must be represented and what the network manager can really use. This information may be expanded with variables that will be of benefit to the testing or service groups. The point to be made is that every variable that can be represented need not be included. Often the size of the MIB is almost viewed as a statement about the quality of the equipment. Nothing could be further from the truth. In most cases a large MIB ends up containing excess baggage that will at some point be dropped anyway.

As the data is gathered, you must also develop the data relations. For example, the relations of the data for a phone switch can determine how the communications cards get represented in the MIB. To determine whether the cards are an element of a row in a card rack or whether they are an element related to a product you must have some notion of the data relations. Some slots in the rack may be empty or use different cards that are not network cards; how should this be represented in the MIB? This interrelation between rack, card, and slot must be depicted in the MIB. Remember, the way this information is represented in the MIB as DOT notation must make some kind of sense. This becomes much like normalizing a database. Many times a database person can be of real assistance in creating these relations.

In a real world case, a client built its MIB such that it represented the slot in a rack by the card in the slot. The client had forgotten that a slot could be empty so the configuration would not continue until a card type was entered. The configuration would then force the user to enter configuration data. The system would hang when it tried to apply the configuration to a card slot that was empty.

The MIB structure and relations can be very complex. An example of when detailed information should be utilized in a MIB would be with a phone switch. Many phone switches want to provide the ability to set up rules for the phone lines. The rules are information telling the phone switch to do things like gather touch tones or generate a dial tone. The rules can be complex, and no set number of rules is required. Nor is there a set pattern used with the rules. Developers should remember that the MIB includes TRAP information. The MIB may also include what management stations are to receive TRAPs. Traps seem to be an area that does not get enough up-front thought. At first it may seem to be simple but let's consider a case in which the equipment has a temperature setting kept in the MIB, the agent may be structured to send alarms if the temperature is out of range. So what happens when the equipment gets a cold boot? You may see a flurry of alarms, which is not exactly what was intended. The MIB should be constructed with range and initialization values. That will do a great deal to reduce the TRAP problem, but there must also be logic that regulates the number of TRAPs sent. The logic might be constructed such that the agent will only repeat a TRAP every so many seconds. This logic has to be analyzed giving thought to the connectionless nature of the protocol. If the period between sending TRAPs is too long and the TRAPs are not getting through, a serious problem may go unattended.

Extensible MIB/Agent

All the vendors made a good effort to ensure that the agent MIB could be extended (extensible) and that information could be conveyed to the management station. Extensibility has merit in a world of embedded systems, such extensibility may be of little value. After all, how many routers will ever extend the MIB. Such extensibility is far more important on the management platform. In the management environment the agent MIB extensions are placed in a file structure. That can be impossible on an embedded system that does not have a file system. The extensibility is much more appropriate on the management station.

MIB History

The first MIB, called MIB I, was described in RFC 1156 and published in 1990. This MIB got divided into 8 groups—System, Interfaces, Address Translation, IP, ICMP, TCP, UDP, and EGP. MIB I has been replaced by elements of the Concise MIB. Proprietary MIBs have been forthcoming, but they are not at all of the quality that one would hope for. Most of them seem to be very simple and often they do not even cover the elements that would be important to a network manager. Very few MIB developers ever ask themselves "what does a network manager need to be able to manage this equipment?" All too often they will provide meaningless counters and other things that the network manager probably will never look at and does not care about.

THE ENTERPRISE MIB

As pointed out earlier, the MIB development is the heart of an SNMP implementation. The MIB must be consistent with both the objects and format of the MIB standards.

Hundreds of vendors have implemented MIBs yet only some are published. Vendors generally provide an MIB to their clients only. This selective distribution of a MIB can end in some strange scenarios. While it can limit the chances that changes will take place without the end user/client receiving the changes, often there is a request on the Internet for a MIB. This is a real problem since simply acquiring an MIB that is made by the vendor for a particular piece of equipment does not guarantee that it will work. For example, if the vendor has updated the platform to support SNMP and there is just a different revision level for the SNMP version, the person who acquired an MIB via the Internet may call the vendor and asks "why doesn't the SNMP work on my system?" The vendor then has to jump through hoops to determine what is going on. Users should always go to the vendor for the correct MIB, but there is no way to enforce such a policy so the problem is sure to continue.

Below is a small section of an MIB that has had the names changed to protect the innocent. It provides a small look at a client's MIB. This MIB was based upon TEMPLATES that readily compile on HP OpenView. There are many differences between compilers, and you should develop your MIB/SMI coding so that it can be used by as many compilers as possible. Although this MIB will compiler on HP OpenView, PEER, and others, it will not compile on SNMPc which is a very popular product. This can become an issue for vendors if it is not addressed with some consistent policy. If you are using an agent that provides a compiler with extensions to help development, you will probably want to utilize those extensions, provided your MIB can also be delivered without the extensions for your clients. An example of this is the case of the HP compiler which will allow you to define ACCESS functions that will provide stub call lines to assist the programmer. These extensions, on some compilers, will cause real problems in the form of compiler errors.

A real-world example of SMI code is presented below.

```
— Card summary (ref: 2.2.1)
— ==============================
— Create a table of slots for the equipment rack
— The table is created under "system 1" - this allows
— the vendor to develop multiple pieces of equipment
— using different MIB's all under the vendor's id.

xyzSlotTable  OBJECT-TYPE
      SYNTAX  SEQUENCE OF XyzSlotEntry
      ACCESS  not-accessible
      STATUS  mandatory
      DESCRIPTION
             "This table contains an entry for each slot on the XYZ
              system. Each entry uniquely identifies the physical
              position of a card."
      ::= {systems 1}

— Below we expand the table to further identify the card, rack and slot

xyzSlotEntry  OBJECT-TYPE
      SYNTAX  XyzSlotEntry
      ACCESS  not-accessible
```

```
                STATUS  mandatory
                DESCRIPTION
                        "Each entry contains the rack (R), level (L)
                        and the slot# (S) identifier which uniquely
                        identifies the position of the card."
                INDEX   { xyzSlotIndex }
                ::= { xyzSlotTable 1 }

        XyzSlotEntry ::=
                SEQUENCE {
                        xyzSlotIndex    INTEGER,
                        xyzSlotRack     INTEGER,
                        xyzSlotLevel    INTEGER,
                        xyzSlotNumber   INTEGER
                        }


        xyzSlotIndex   OBJECT-TYPE
                SYNTAX  INTEGER
                ACCESS  read-only
                        C_STRUCT row, FIELD description
                STATUS  mandatory
                DESCRIPTION
                        "This is the key to the accompany XyzSlotTable,
                        identifies the card for which a entry exists."
                ::= { xyzSlotEntry 1 }

        xyzSlotRack    OBJECT-TYPE
                SYNTAX  INTEGER
                ACCESS  read-only
                        C_STRUCT row, FIELD description
                STATUS  mandatory
                DESCRIPTION
                        "Identifies the rack."
                ::= { xyzSlotEntry 2 }

        xyzSlotLevel   OBJECT-TYPE
                SYNTAX  INTEGER
                ACCESS  read-only
                        C_STRUCT row, FIELD description
                STATUS  mandatory
                ::= { xyzSlotEntry 3 }

        xyzSlotNumber  OBJECT-TYPE
                SYNTAX  INTEGER
                ACCESS  read-only
                        C_STRUCT row, FIELD description
                STATUS  mandatory
                ::= { xyzSlotEntry 4 }
```

```
xyzCardType   OBJECT-TYPE
    SYNTAX  INTEGER
    ACCESS  read-only
            C_VARIABLE atype
    STATUS  mandatory
    DESCRIPTION
            "Identifies the slot number."
    ::= { xyzSlotEntry 4 }
```

All of the definitions above provide information relating to the contents of a card cage. It allows, through the use of a table, the structuring of data into rows and columns—a table.

MIB Definition

For a MIB to be of value to various management platforms there needed to be a consistent method for definition of objects. The consistency of the MIB module is addressed in RFC 1212. Prior to RFC 1212 there were two methods of defining objects: a textural definition and using ASN.1 OBJECT-TYPE macros.

The OBJECT-TYPE Macro is constructed of several elements:

- SYNTAX—defines the data structure of an object.

- ACCESS—defines the access of the object—for example: read-only, read-write or not-accessible.

- STATUS—defines the implementation requirements of the object. It may be optional, obsolete, etc.

- DESCRIPTION—may or may not be present. Provides a textural definition.

- INDEX—used with the row objects only.

- DEFVAL—optional, is used to populate values of column objects.

RFC 1212 provides for a textural definition within the OBJECT-TYPE macro, thus reducing the amount of documentation required internally. Unfortunately this does not resolve the issue of user documentation. The user is the client who will eventually get your MIB. The user will generally need a hardcopy that gives him or her a good deal more information than will be contained in the documentation area of the MIB. The hardcopy should provide the user with some understanding of the MIB as a whole as well as information about how the data interrelates. For example, if SNMP Variable X should never be set without SNMP variable Y being set first, this protocol must be conveyed to the user/client. All too often, vendors will not provide sufficient detail for the MIB variables to be of value. If the name of the MIB variable does not sufficiently explain the variable and the documentation is lacking, the variable has no value to the user.

Even the standards leave ambiguity, such as "uptime." What is uptime, how long the system has been up? No, it is how long SNMP has been active. Nothing specifically to do with the system.

The OBJECT-TYPE macro utilized in a MIB would take the form shown in the example below.

The example is taken from the compilation of MIB.

```
— the System group
— Implementation of the System group is mandatory for all
— systems.  If an agent is not configured to have a value
— for any of these variables, a string of length 0 is
— returned.

sysDescr OBJECT-TYPE
    SYNTAX  DisplayString (SIZE (0..255))
    ACCESS  read-only
    STATUS  mandatory
    DESCRIPTION
            "A textual description of the entity.  This value
            should include the full name and version
            identification of the system's hardware type,
            software operating-system, and networking
            software.  It is mandatory that this only contain
            printable ASCII characters."
    ::= { system 1 }


sysObjectID OBJECT-TYPE
    SYNTAX  OBJECT IDENTIFIER
    PROMPT "network management subsystem i'd"
    ACCESS  read-only
    STATUS  mandatory
    DESCRIPTION
            "The vendor's authoritative identification of the
            network management subsystem contained in the
            entity.  This value is allocated within the SMI
            enterprises subtree (1.3.6.1.4.1) and provides an
            easy and unambiguous means for determining `what
            kind of box' is being managed.
    ::= { system 2 }

sysUpTime OBJECT-TYPE
    SYNTAX  TimeTicks
    PROMPT "System Up time"
    ACCESS  read-only
    STATUS  mandatory
    DESCRIPTION
            "The time (in hundredths of a second) since the
            network management portion of the system was last
            re-initialized."
    ::= { system 3 }
```

These elements of the SMI are elements contained in the standard MIB and are variables that should be contained in every MIB at some level. Often it is sufficient for a MIB to import this information. That is done through the use of an IMPORT statement in the MIB.

An example of using IMPORT with a MIB is presented below.

```
RFC1213-MIB DEFINITIONS ::= BEGIN

IMPORTS
        mgmt, NetworkAddress, IpAddress, Counter, Gauge, TimeTicks
             FROM RFC1155-SMI
        OBJECT-TYPE
             FROM RFC-1212;

—  This MIB module uses the extended OBJECT-TYPE macro as
—  defined in [14];


—  MIB-II (same prefix as MIB-I)

mib-2      OBJECT IDENTIFIER ::= { mgmt 1 }

Taken from MIB II  SMI.
```

The OID (Object ID)

The private MIB gets implemented on a branch of the Object IDentifier (OID) tree. If the developer intends to utilize any proprietary data in the MIB he or she will need to have a branch on the MIB tree that defines the enterprise. The enterprise can gain a number specific to his or her organization by contacting:

IANA (Internet Assigned Numbers Authority)
Joe Kemp USC/ISI
Voice 310-822-1511 ext. 171
Fax 310-823-6714
E-mail: IANA-MIB @ isi.EDU

Every organization that intends to develop in the SNMP world will probably want its own number. The assigned number will be in the 1200 range by the time this is published. This number provides a location on a search tree that is unique to a specific organization. A developer may want to apply for a number while he or she begins the MIB data collection process. The number only takes a few days to get and requires only a minimal amount of information about the organization.

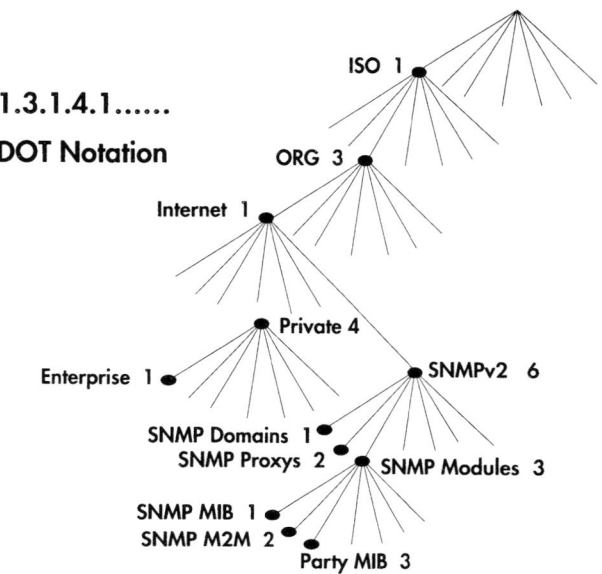

Figure 5.1 The OID Tree.

Additional information about existing private MIBs can be acquired, on the Internet, from Venera.isi.edu, directory MIB. A file of special interest is snmp-vendors-contacts, which lists currently-assigned private enterprise codes. Many private MIBs are included in this directory. The information in this file and directory can also provide insight about the various organizations that provide some type of SNMP product or support.

At this point, the reader should be looking into the data required to create a MIB, thinking about the organization of the data, and have at least applied for an ID number. Having all of that in place, the work of creating the SMI code should begin. Do not go into this thinking that the first cut will be the last. The effort of organizing the SMI and the data relations can become an ongoing effort. It may be that you will begin your SMI encoding and continue with your agent development. As the agent progresses, it will be easier to determine what changes would be important to the SMI code.

ASN.1, BER, AND DER (ABSTRACT SYNTAX NOTATION ONE, BASIC ENCODING RULES, AND DISTINGUISHED ENCODING RULES)

As one might believe, ASN.1, BER, and DER are all related to a degree. ASN.1 defines an abstract notation that allows data to be described without concern for how it is actually implemented. This allows each hardware platform to use the most appropriate technique to implement the rules. ASN.1 uses types to describe the data, and BER describes how to represent those types. DER is a subset of BER that gives a unique encoding to each ASN.1 value.

ASN.1 Terminology and Notation

ASN.1 uses octets as a descriptor. An octet being 8-bits with bit 8 the most significant bit and bit 1 is the least significant. ASN.1 uses the following meta syntax:

- BIT   monospace denotes literal characters
- n1   italics denotes variables
- []   brackets indicate that a term is optional
- {}   braces group related terms
- | bar delimits alternatives
- ...   ellipsis indicate repeated occurrences
- =   equals sign expresses terms as sub-terms

ASN.1 uses type fields with some fields using tags. The fields CHOICE and ANY do not use tags while all others do. The four tag classes are:

- universal—used for types whose meaning is the same in all applications
- application—for types specific to an application
- private—for types specific to an enterprise
- context-specific—for types specific to their usage

ASN.1 encoding could be made into a book of its own, and further study should be given to the encoding rules. Much material is available on the subject including several International Standards Organization (ISO) documents.

BER Terminology and Notation

BER provides three ways to describe ASN.1 values as octet strings. The three methods are:

- primitive—definite length encoding
- constructed—definite length encoding and constructed
- constructed—indefinite length

An explanation of the workings of BER is beyond the scope of this book. Any number of documents which do that are available. The important factor is to have a definition of the terms, since they are often used without explanation.

Each of the BER encoding methods has three or four parts:

- **Identifier octets**—these identify the class and tag number

- **Length octets**—for definite length methods these define the number of octets contained. For constructed these indicate the length of indefinite.

- **Contents octets**—for primitive these provide a representation of the value. For constructed these provide a concatenation of the BER encoding of the component value.

- **End-of-contents octets**—for constructed methods these denote the end of contents. For other methods these are absent.

DER Terminology and Notation

DER encoding provides for a subset of the BER encoding. It is not utilized or discussed to the degree that BER encoding is, and it will not be reviewed here. The specific rules of DER encoding are available in many documents and are available from many sources.

The encoding rules become more important for those attempting to debug the protocol than for those trying to use an existing package. Any package worth having will have all of those issues resolved. Of course if you are developing an agent from scratch, you will want to understand the DER encoding.

INTERNALS

Some of the issues that are touched on in this section greatly differ between V1 and V2. The reader is cautioned to refer to the latest appropriate RFC for clarification as well as for specific requirements. The reader should monitor the discussions on the Internet. A good deal of knowledge can be gained from these discussions. You need not comment, but most readers will have questions that can be answered by those who monitor these groups.

Internal Data Representation

In the last chapter we looked at the SMI data representation. Here we take a look at the agents view of the data. It must be understood that the data can be represented differently from one SNMP agent to the next, but the most common representation is the use of a balanced tree structure. The B-Tree is a common data processing methodology that is well documented elsewhere, and we will not go into it in detail here.

NOTE: BTree software is included on the accompanying diskette.

It should be noted that some compilers and agents will allow various data bases to be interfaced via the MIB and MIB compiler. Those that allow the MIB compiler to interact with a database will provide calls directly to the data base Standard Query Language (SQL). A number of agents will use a simple B-Tree to contain the MIB elements. The OIDs will be stored in the tree. When the agent needs to find an OID, it will search the nodes on the tree using the OID for the search criteria. If the node is found, the OID is valid, and so on. There is generally logic in the agent to convert OID to a type or a textural name to OID. These conversions will allow the B-Tree to store the values in various ways. Each tree node will contain a structure that will utilize a structure to hold the type, value and length fields. There may be additional material contained in these structures. Generally, agents are created such that the structure can be modified (enlarged) without changes to the agent code. Such changes can be done to allow the structures to contain pointers to functions and other material. The function pointers can be utilized to access functions that do calculations, gather data, or do any of a number of other things that may become important for providing good quality data. CMIP provides the capability for such functions. They are called ACTIONS, and it is clear that such action capability can greatly enhance network management capability. SNMP did not provide as elegant an operation as ACTIONS, yet with a little creativity and understanding the same effect can be had.

Many vendors currently offer an interface to at least one commercial database. HP plans to offer a generic database interface this year. This allows the use of a database to store the MIB data doing data retrievals by normal database calls. Unfortunately, an intelligent data cache is impossible to build and most of the data must be retrieved or calculated each time it is accessed.

Table Access

Another element that is internal to the agent is table access. SNMP requires that a table mechanism be available. Most commercial agents will have the objects for a table created and ready to go. Developers creating SNMP agents from scratch or using one of the public domain agents may have to create the table mechanism.

SNMP also requires that the agent be able to add and delete rows from the table. The agent must be able to add a row with a SET operation. It must also be able to delete a row with a SET operation. The exact mechanics of how the agent does this is a matter for the implementor, and generally the mechanics are specific to a given agent. Often an agent will simply mark a row as not valid and not delete the row and that is acceptable, since the RFCs do not specify the mechanism for doing the deletion. Many agents and most management stations will utilize the MIB to provide the OBJECTs for table rows. The structures for a table are presented below. Another interesting element of the compiler output shown below is that it comes from the SMI encoding above (see the Enterprise MIB section previously described in this chapter).

```
/*******************************************************************************
 * The OID (DOT NOTATION) is carried in the ubyte below. A ubyte is simply a
 * common name that is a type specific to the hardware it is utilized on.
 *******************************************************************************/

static ubyte  ATTR_ID_ASN_xyzCardType [] =
      {
      0x80, 0x0d, 0x2b, 0x06, 0x01, 0x04, 0x01, 0x86, 0x76, 0x01, 0x01, 0x01,
      0x04, 0x01, 0x00,
      };
static struct object_id      ATTR_ID_xyzCardType = {
      15,
      ATTR_ID_ASN_xyzCardType,
};


/*******************************************************************************
 * The function below is generated by the MIB compiler as a stub. This
 * particular stub will provide all the material needed. Most stubs will need
 * to be fleshed out by the programmer.
 *
 * This stub returns the card type from a type field contained in the
 * structure. The type must have been filled in elsewhere, possibility during
 * an initialization or by another piece of code in the host application.

 *******************************************************************************/
static int
SNMP_GET_xyzCardType(ctxt, indices, attr)
void              *ctxt;
void              **indices;
INTEGER           *attr;
      {
      *attr = ((struct if_row_context *)ctxt)->type;
      return(SNMP_ERR_NO_ERROR);
      }


extern int              SNMP_GET_xyzCardType();
static struct attribute ATTR_xyzCardType =
      {
      &ATTR_ID_xyzCardType,
```

```
        SNMP_GET_xyzCardType,
        NULL,
        NULL,
        NULL,
        NULL,
        NULL,
        3,                /* INTEGER */
        -2147483648,
        2147483647,
        };
/***************************************************************************
 * Card status is a reply of card type above. It can be noted that the code
 * generated for the status is not correct. This would indicate that the SMI
 * used to generate the code was not correct. Just as with any code the
 * compiler will generate code that is worthless if it gets bad input.

 ***************************************************************************/
static ubyte  ATTR_ID_ASN_xyzCardStatus [] =
        {
        0x80, 0x0d, 0x2b, 0x06, 0x01, 0x04, 0x01, 0x86, 0x76, 0x01, 0x01, 0x01,
        0x04, 0x01, 0x00,
        };

static struct object_id      ATTR_ID_xyzCardStatus = {
        15,
        ATTR_ID_ASN_xyzCardStatus,
};


static int
SNMP_GET_xyzCardStatus(ctxt, indices, attr)
void                *ctxt;
void                **indices;
INTEGER             *attr;
        {
        *attr = ((struct if_row_context *)ctxt)->type;
        return(SNMP_ERR_NO_ERROR);
        }

/*ARGSUSED*/
static int
SNMP_SET_xyzCardStatus(ctxt, indices, attr)
void                *ctxt;
void                **indices;
INTEGER             *attr;
        {
        ((struct if_row_context *)ctxt)->type = *attr;
        return(SNMP_ERR_NO_ERROR);
        }

extern int          SNMP_GET_xyzCardStatus();
```

```
extern int              SNMP_SET_xyzCardStatus();
static struct attribute ATTR_xyzCardStatus =
      {
      &ATTR_ID_xyzCardStatus,
      SNMP_GET_xyzCardStatus,
      SNMP_SET_xyzCardStatus,
      NULL,
      NULL,
      NULL,
      NULL,
      3,              /* INTEGER */
      -2147483648,
      2147483647,
      };

static ubyte  ATTR_ID_ASN_xyzUnusedPorts [] =
      {
      0x80, 0x0d, 0x2b, 0x06, 0x01, 0x04, 0x01, 0x86, 0x76, 0x01, 0x01, 0x01,
      0x04, 0x02, 0x00,
      };

static struct object_id     ATTR_ID_xyzUnusedPorts = {
      15,
      ATTR_ID_ASN_xyzUnusedPorts,
};

/*ARGSUSED*/
static int
SNMP_GET_xyzUnusedPorts(ctxt, indices, attr)
void              *ctxt;
void              **indices;
INTEGER           *attr;
      {
      *attr = ((struct ports *)ctxt)->portNum;
      return(SNMP_ERR_NO_ERROR);
      }

/*ARGSUSED*/
static int
SNMP_SET_xyzUnusedPorts(ctxt, indices, attr)
void              *ctxt;
void              **indices;
INTEGER           *attr;
      {
      ((struct ports *)ctxt)->portNum = *attr;
      return(SNMP_ERR_NO_ERROR);
      }
```

```
/**************************************************************************
 * The code also keeps track of the ports, both used and unused. Note that
 * the code uses a call to an external function to provide this information.
 * The external calls return an integer which is the number of ports.

 **************************************************************************/
extern int          SNMP_GET_xyzUnusedPorts();
extern int          SNMP_SET_xyzUnusedPorts();
extern void         *xyzUnusedPorts();
static struct attribute ATTR_xyzUnusedPorts =
      {
      &ATTR_ID_xyzUnusedPorts,
      SNMP_GET_xyzUnusedPorts,
      SNMP_SET_xyzUnusedPorts,
      NULL,
      NULL,
      xyzUnusedPorts,
      NULL,
      3,                /* INTEGER */
      -2147483648,
      2147483647,
      };
/**************************************************************************
 * Here is an array of structures (a table) that  contains the card type,
 * status and number of unused ports. The function above that returned status
 * should have referenced the status field. It should also be noted that used
 * ports are not kept. Used ports can be calculated given unused ports.

 **************************************************************************/
static struct attribute *ATTRS_xyzSlotNumber [] =
      {
      &ATTR_xyzCardType,
      &ATTR_xyzCardStatus,
      &ATTR_xyzUnusedPorts,
      NULL
      };

static ubyte  GROUP_ID_ASN_xyzSlotNumber [] =
      {
      0x80, 0x0b, 0x2b, 0x06, 0x01, 0x04, 0x01, 0x86, 0x76, 0x01, 0x01, 0x01,
      0x04,
      };

static struct object_id     GROUP_ID_xyzSlotNumber = {
      13,
      GROUP_ID_ASN_xyzSlotNumber,
};

struct class_definition     SMI_GROUP_xyzSlotNumber =
      {
      SNMP_CLASS,
```

```
            &GROUP_ID_xyzSlotNumber,
            ATTRS_xyzSlotNumber,
            NULL,
            NULL,
            NULL,
            NULL,
            NULL,
            NULL,
            NULL,
            NULL,
            NULL,
            };

struct contained_obj CONT_GROUP_xyzSlotNumber = {
        &SMI_GROUP_xyzSlotNumber,
        NULL
};

static ubyte  ATTR_ID_ASN_lcPortIndex [] =
        {
        0x80, 0x0e, 0x2b, 0x06, 0x01, 0x04, 0x01, 0x86, 0x76, 0x01, 0x01, 0x01,
        0x01, 0x01, 0x01, 0x01,
        };

static struct object_id        ATTR_ID_lcPortIndex = {
        16,
        ATTR_ID_ASN_lcPortIndex,
}


/****************************************************************************
 * Below we have a port index used. The port index can be used as a reference
 * into the port table.

 ****************************************************************************/
static int
SNMP_GET_lcPortIndex(ctxt, indices, attr)
void               *ctxt;
void               **indices;
INTEGER            *attr;
        {
        *attr = ((struct system_context *)ctxt)->description;
        return (SNMP_ERR_NO_ERROR);
        }

extern int         SNMP_GET_lcPortIndex();
extern struct attribute *INDEXES_lcPortEntry[];
static struct attribute ATTR_lcPortIndex =
        {
        &ATTR_ID_lcPortIndex,
        SNMP_GET_lcPortIndex,
```

```
      NULL,
      NULL,
      NULL,
      NULL,
      &INDEXES_lcPortEntry[0],
      3,              /* INTEGER */
#define MIN_lcPortIndex        1
      MIN_lcPortIndex,

#define MAX_lcPortIndex        8
      MAX_lcPortIndex,
      };

static ubyte  ATTR_ID_ASN_lcPortName [] =
      {
      0x80, 0x0e, 0x2b, 0x06, 0x01, 0x04, 0x01, 0x86, 0x76, 0x01, 0x01, 0x01,
      0x01, 0x01, 0x01, 0x02,
      };

static struct object_id        ATTR_ID_lcPortName = {
      16,
      ATTR_ID_ASN_lcPortName,
};

/*ARGSUSED*/
static int
SNMP_GET_lcPortName(ctxt, indices, attr)
void              *ctxt;
void              **indices;
OCTETSTRING       *attr;
      {
      *attr = ((struct system_context *)ctxt)->uptime;
      return(SNMP_ERR_NO_ERROR);
      }


/*ARGSUSED*/
static int
SNMP_SET_lcPortName(ctxt, indices, attr)
void              *ctxt;
void              **indices;
OCTETSTRING       *attr;
      {
      ((struct system_context *)ctxt)->uptime.len = attr->len;
      bcopy(attr->val, ((struct system_context *)ctxt)->uptime.val,
                  attr->len);
      return(SNMP_ERR_NO_ERROR);
      }

extern int         SNMP_GET_lcPortName();
extern int         SNMP_SET_lcPortName();
extern void        *calc_system_uptime();
```

```
extern struct attribute *INDEXES_lcPortEntry[];
static struct attribute ATTR_lcPortName =
        {
        &ATTR_ID_lcPortName,
        SNMP_GET_lcPortName,
        SNMP_SET_lcPortName,
        NULL,
        NULL,
        calc_system_uptime,
        &INDEXES_lcPortEntry[0],
        1,                  /* OCTETSTRING */
#define MIN_lcPortName       0
        MIN_lcPortName,
#define MAX_lcPortName       8
        MAX_lcPortName,
        };
```

In the compiler output above, the references to indices relates to the table indexing. This particular compiler output was part of a step-wise refinement of the SMI/MIB. To take full advantage of the material an understanding of "C," structures and pointers will be required. The output above has taken several pages for a small example; a large MIB can take hundreds of pages and thousands of lines of code. The example above was limited to the most relevant parts. It should be examined carefully since the interrelations are subtle.

FOR FURTHER STUDY

The following documents contain useful information that is beyond the scope of this chapter.

Kaliski, Jr. Burton. *A Layman's Guide to a Subset of ASN.1*, "White Paper—RSA Data Security," Inc., Redwood, CA. (A must BER, and DER.)

Perkins, David. *Understanding SNMP MIBs White Paper*. July 7, 1992. (A MUST!)

REFERENCES

Galvin, J. and McCloghrie, K. *Internet request for comment Security Protocols for version 2 of the Simple Network Management V2*. RFC 1446, April 1993.

Perkins, David. *Understanding SNMP MIBs White Paper*. July 7, 1992.

6

The MIB

INTRODUCTION

We have talked about the need to gather the data to create the SMI and the MIB but we have avoided the detail of how to create the SMI/MIB. Reading the RFCs relating to the MIB and SMI coding can be somewhat intimidating. At best, it is difficult to understand. I will try to provide some simple explanation of the how and why of creating SMI/MIB in this chapter. Some of the material will not get the coverage it deserves. To provide that level of detail would require a book, not a chapter. A more complete presentation of SMI usage and MIB creation can be gained from the booklet done by David Perkins entitled *Understanding SNMP MIBs*. It is an excellent work by any standard.

MIB GROUPINGS

By this time you have heard the term MIB, but what does it really refer to? Well, it can refer to different things depending on the context. When reading this material, the context should be considered in evaluating the term MIB. SNMP utilizes the managed data in somewhat a conventional database mentality. Some wrongfully refer to the MIB as a "database" although for all intent and purpose it is a database. When in machine memory, the MIB variables can be dynamically allocated only as needed. The dynamic allocation helps to conserve memory. This model goes against the conventional database model so it is not considered to be a database.

Many MIBs include (IMPORT) standard MIBs to have access to the standard groups. When a standard group contains some objects that are applicable to your implementation you IMPORT that MIB. When using a standard MIB not all groups of the MIB need be implemented; but all objects of the groups used must be implemented to claim compliance. This can become an issue for equipment that does not support some of the MIB elements.

MIB II provides six basic groups, they are:

1. SNMPv2 Statistics Group

   Objects that provide basic instruction of the SNMPv2 entity. An example is packets received, authentication errors, etc.

2. SNMPv1 Statistics Group

   Objects that provide basic instrumentation of the SNMPv2 entity that also implements SNMPv1; for example, community name.

3. Object Resource Group

   Objects that allow an SNMPv2 entity acting in an agent role to describe its dynamically-configurable objects.

4. Trap Group

   Objects that allow the SNMPv2 entity, when acting in an agent role to be configured to generate TRAP PDUs.

5. Well-Known Traps Group

   Objects that describe the six well-known traps from SNMPv1:

   - coldStart
   - warmStart
   - linkDown
   - linkUp
   - authenticationFailure
   - egpNeighborLoss

6. The Set Group

   Objects that allow several, cooperating, SNMPv2 entities all acting in a manager role to coordinate their use with the SNMPv2 Set operation. Functioning similar to a "locking" mechanism.

OBJECT IDS

The objects in the MIB get assigned an object id (OID), unique to that object. OIDs are non negative integers that get organized in a hierarchical ordering. The OID is assigned a textural name to help the human interpretation. The DOT notation (Figure 6.1) positions the object in the object tree. OIDs are written in the following formats:

```
SYNTAX
"{"  {{<name>["("<number>")"]} | <number>} ..... "}"
                or
<number> ["."<number>].....
Where
<name> is a component name;
              and
<number> is a component value.
```

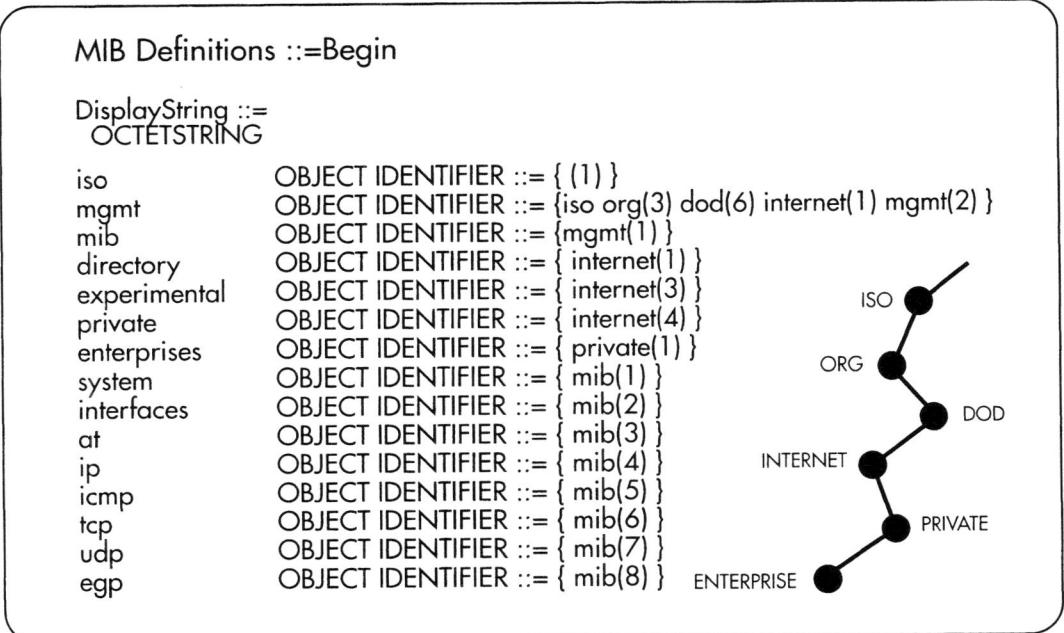

```
MIB Definitions ::=Begin

DisplayString ::=
    OCTETSTRING

iso             OBJECT IDENTIFIER ::= { (1) }
mgmt            OBJECT IDENTIFIER ::= {iso org(3) dod(6) internet(1) mgmt(2) }
mib             OBJECT IDENTIFIER ::= {mgmt(1) }
directory       OBJECT IDENTIFIER ::= { internet(1) }
experimental    OBJECT IDENTIFIER ::= { internet(3) }
private         OBJECT IDENTIFIER ::= { internet(4) }
enterprises     OBJECT IDENTIFIER ::= { private(1) }
system          OBJECT IDENTIFIER ::= { mib(1) }
interfaces      OBJECT IDENTIFIER ::= { mib(2) }
at              OBJECT IDENTIFIER ::= { mib(3) }
ip              OBJECT IDENTIFIER ::= { mib(4) }
icmp            OBJECT IDENTIFIER ::= { mib(5) }
tcp             OBJECT IDENTIFIER ::= { mib(6) }
udp             OBJECT IDENTIFIER ::= { mib(7) }
egp             OBJECT IDENTIFIER ::= { mib(8) }
```

Figure 6.1 OID Tree.

Along with the tree, above it is important to see that translated into the actual SMI implementation presented on the following page.

```
system         OBJECT IDENTIFIER ::= { mib-2 1 }
interfaces     OBJECT IDENTIFIER ::= { mib-2 2 }
at             OBJECT IDENTIFIER ::= { mib-2 3 }
ip             OBJECT IDENTIFIER ::= { mib-2 4 }
icmp           OBJECT IDENTIFIER ::= { mib-2 5 }
tcp            OBJECT IDENTIFIER ::= { mib-2 6 }
udp            OBJECT IDENTIFIER ::= { mib-2 7 }
egp            OBJECT IDENTIFIER ::= { mib-2 8 }
```

The lines above define an object identifier for each of the elements in the left hand column. It provides a relation of the OBJECT with its parent, the object on the right—in this case mib-2.

```
— historical (some say hysterical)
— cmot      OBJECT IDENTIFIER ::= { mib-2 9 }
transmission OBJECT IDENTIFIER ::= { mib-2 10 }
snmp OBJECT IDENTIFIER ::= { mib-2 11 }
```

As this step-by-step relation gets down to the portion of the MIB that relates to the specific equipment to be managed, the objects at the level of the specific vendor equipment are said to be "ENTERPRISE"-specific. The ENTERPRISE-particular dot (node) on the tree references the specific number assigned to the vendor organization by IANA. The accepted approach is to have additional nodes under the enterprise node. These additional nodes provide for areas that can be used for individual products, test areas, and so on.

The naming convention used in this enterprise MIB is that, if the development is intended to become IEFT () standard MIB, the names must be unique. For experimental and proprietary MIBs this requirement is not and could not be enforced.

STRUCTURED MANAGEMENT INFORMATION (SMI)

SMI describes how to use a subset of ASN.1 to define an information module. Other restrictions are placed on "standard" information modules as well. It is strongly recommended that "enterprise-specific" information modules also adhere to these restrictions, although it cannot be enforced.

SMI is a set of conventions that are set out in the Internet documents and elsewhere. The types, allowed within the guidelines set forth by SMI are:

```
Primitive Types
- INTEGER
- OCTET STRING
- OBJECT IDENTIFIER
- NULL
Constructor Types
```

```
- SEQUENCE
- SEQUENCE of
```

(The SMI templates used in this book comply with "Draft Proposal of SMI Part 4—Guidelines for the Definition of Managed Object" ISO/IEC 10165-4.)

Defined Types

Only the ASN.1 primitive types are permitted. These are referred to as non-aggregate types. Enumerated INTEGERS can be utilized, but when they are, a named number with a value of 0 must not be present in the list of enumerations.

Constructor Types

Sequence constructor type is permitted, providing that it is used to generate either lists or tables.

For lists, the syntax takes the form:

```
SEQUENCE { <typel>, ..., <type N> >
```

where each <type> resolves to one of the primitive types listed. DEFAULT and OPTIONAL types can not appear in the sequence definition.

For tables, the syntax takes the form:

```
SEQUENCE OF <entry>
```

where <entry> resolves to a list constructor.

Lists and tables are often known as aggregate types.

Defined Types

In addition, new application-wide types may be defined, so long as they resolve into implicitly defined ASN.1 primitive types. There are few defined types at this time. Most of the implementations are content to utilize MIB II and RMON, the buzz words. Yet some vendors wish to supply additional types to make for a more intelligent MIB. After all the MIB is the definition of the data within the system. If that data is to represent some complex knowledge, it may require more than the basic types.

It is important to understand that there are also ASN.1 compilers available. These compilers deal with straight ASN.1 code without the conversion to the SMI format. These compilers tend to be utilized with ISO software more than with the SNMP software.

A strict ASN.1 compiler may be used with an ISO protocol stack to generate code for a user application. It would provide all the calls required to interface with the host BEDL (Basic Encoding/Decoding Libraries).

Using SMI to Create the MIB

At this point you may find yourself thoroughly confused. Don't feel bad; SMI ASN.1, BER and DER can all start to run together. We will make an effort to put it together in a manner that is easier to deal with. While the exact specifications can be found in the following documents.

- *Concise MIB format*—RFC1212: by M. Rose and S. McCloghrie
- *Structure of Management Information*—RFC1442: by J. Case, K. McCloghrie, M. Rose, and S. Waldbusser
- *Trap format*—RFC1215; by M. Rose

SMI Encoding Components

Standard Management Information is a subset of ASN.1 and observes the related keywords. Some of them are:

- BEGIN
- DEFINED
- DEFINITIONS
- END
- EXPORTS
- IDENTIFIER
- IMPORTS
- INTEGER
- NULL
- OBJECT
- OCTET
- OF
- SEQUENCE
- STRING

SMI is divided into three parts: module definitions, object definitions, and trap definitions.

(1) Module definitions are used when describing the semantics of an information module.

(2) Object definitions are used when describing the syntax and semantics of a managed object.

(3) Notification definitions are used when describing unsolicited management information.

These parts are used to create the SMI encoding. A short example is presented below. The example is the TCP portion of the a standard MIB. It represents the use of the various components of SMI encoding.

```
— the TCP group

tcpRtoAlgorithm OBJECT-TYPE
        SYNTAX  INTEGER {
        other(1),    — none of the following
        constant(2), — a constant rte
        rsre(3),     — MIL-STD-1778, Appendix B
        vanj(4)      — Van Jacobson's algorithm [11]
                }
        ACCESS  read-only
        STATUS  mandatory
        ::= { tcp 1 }

tcpRtoMin OBJECT-TYPE
        SYNTAX  INTEGER
        ACCESS  read-only
        STATUS  mandatory
        ::= { tcp 2 }

tcpRtoMax OBJECT-TYPE
        SYNTAX  INTEGER
        ACCESS  read-only
        STATUS  mandatory
        ::= { tcp 3 }

tcpMaxConn OBJECT-TYPE
        SYNTAX  INTEGER
        ACCESS  read-only
        STATUS  mandatory
        ::= { tcp 4 }

tcpActiveOpens OBJECT-TYPE
        SYNTAX  Counter
        ACCESS  read-only
        STATUS  mandatory
        ::= { tcp 5 }
```

```
tcpPassiveOpens OBJECT-TYPE
        SYNTAX  Counter
        ACCESS  read-only
        STATUS  mandatory
        ::= { tcp 6 }

tcpAttemptFails OBJECT-TYPE
        SYNTAX  Counter
        ACCESS  read-only
        STATUS  mandatory
        ::= { tcp 7 }

tcpEstabResets OBJECT-TYPE
        SYNTAX  Counter
        ACCESS  read-only
        STATUS  mandatory
        ::= { tcp 8 }

tcpCurrEstab OBJECT-TYPE
        SYNTAX  Gauge
        ACCESS  read-only
        STATUS  mandatory
        ::= { tcp 9 }

tcpInSegs OBJECT-TYPE
        SYNTAX  Counter
        ACCESS  read-only
        STATUS  mandatory
        ::= { tcp 10 }

tcpOutSegs OBJECT-TYPE
        SYNTAX  Counter
        ACCESS  read-only
        STATUS  mandatory
        ::= { tcp 11 }

tcpRetransSegs OBJECT-TYPE
        SYNTAX  Counter
        ACCESS  read-only
        STATUS  mandatory
        ::= { tcp 12 }

- the TCP connections table

tcpConnTable OBJECT-TYPE
        SYNTAX  SEQUENCE OF TcpConnEntry
        ACCESS  read-only
        STATUS  mandatory
        ::= { tcp 13 }
```

```
tcpConnEntry OBJECT-TYPE
        SYNTAX   TcpConnEntry
        ACCESS   read-only
        STATUS   mandatory
        ::= { tcpConnTable 1 }

TcpConnEntry ::= SEQUENCE {
    tcpConnState
        INTEGER,
    tcpConnLocalAddress
        IpAddress,
    tcpConnLocalPort
        INTEGER (0..65535),
    tcpConnRemAddress
        IpAddress,
    tcpConnRemPort
        INTEGER (0..65535)
}

tcpConnState OBJECT-TYPE
        SYNTAX   INTEGER {
                    closed(1),
                    listen(2),
                    synSent(3),
                    synReceived(4),
                    established(5),
                    finWait1(6),
                    finWait2(7),
                    closeWait(8),
                    lastAck(9),
                    closing(10),
                    timeWait(11)
                 }
        ACCESS   read-only
        STATUS   mandatory
        ::= { tcpConnEntry 1 }

tcpConnLocalAddress OBJECT-TYPE
        SYNTAX   IpAddress
        ACCESS   read-only
        STATUS   mandatory
        ::= { tcpConnEntry 2 }

tcpConnLocalPort OBJECT-TYPE
        SYNTAX   INTEGER (0..65535)
        ACCESS   read-only
        STATUS   mandatory
        ::= { tcpConnEntry 3 }
```

```
tcpConnRemAddress OBJECT-TYPE
          SYNTAX   IpAddress
          ACCESS   read-only
          STATUS   mandatory
          ::= { tcpConnEntry 4 }

tcpConnRemPort OBJECT-TYPE
          SYNTAX   INTEGER (0..65535)
          ACCESS   read-only
          STATUS   mandatory
          ::= { tcpConnEntry 5 }
```

Several complete MIBs are included on the diskettes. Many of the MIBs provided with popular vendor equipment.

Steps to MIB Creation

The steps used in creating a MIB are few but specific. This is a very large part of getting an agent up and functional. The MIB creation should take the steps:

- Gather the variables relevant to the target system.
  (discussed in earlier chapters)

- The first step is to construct a skeletal MIB module.

- Categorize the objects into groups.

- For each managed object class, determine whether there can exist multiple instances of that managed object class. If not, then for each of its attributes, use the OBJECT-TYPE macro to make an equivalent definition. Multiple instances are defined as a conceptual table.

- Begin compiling MIB.

- Refine MIB observing compiler output for correct data relations.

The detail of this process is available in the RFC. As indicated in the RFC, objects are created based on the OBJECT TEMPLATE.

Each entry (object) in the MIB relates to a number in the dot notation. That is to say, the dot notation 1.3.1.6...would be represented by a node with at least three branches, with the third branch having at least six branches and so on. In DOT notation, a scalar object has a 0 (zero) added to the end of the OID. In the case of a columnar entry an index plus a non-zero suffix is added to identify a specific object within a table. For example, to identify the first row, second column we would end the OID with 1.2. The 1 (one) represents the index indicating the first row, and the 2 (two) specifies the second column.

In the case of a table with no rows, the columnar variable in the table is without instance. This means an empty table.

aTable (OID X.X.X.X.X.3.6)						
Row 1	1.1	1.2	1.3	1.4	1.5	1.6
Row 2	2.1	2.2	2.3	2.4	2.5	2.6
Row 3	3.1	3.2	3.3	3.4	3.5	3.6

Figure 6.2 Columnar Example.

Templates

The syntax of SMI can be somewhat complex, and for the complete explanation you should refer to the RFC1212, RFC1442 and ISO/IEC 10165. Below is an example of the template set used by a major SNMP vendor. This particular vendor provides templates that contain enhancements. Such enhancements may not work with other vendors. A developer should utilize templates that are compatible with their agent. The developer should also consider the clients MIB compiler which may not be compatible. It is always safe to utilize a basic template with no enhancements. A study of the MIBs on the accompanying diskettes will provide an understanding of the basic structures.

```
class_label  MANAGED OBJECT CLASS
     [DERIVED FROM   <immediate-superclass-label>
                          [,<immediate-superclass-label>]* :
     ]
     [ALLOMORPHIC SET <class-label> [, <class-label>]* :
     ]
     [CHARACTERIZED BY:
            [BEHAVIOR DEFINITIONS <behavior-def-label>
                               [,<behavior-def-label>]* :
            ]
            [FWSTRUCT TYPE        "<struct xyz>":
            ]
            [ATTRIBUTES <attribute-label><propertylist>
                             [FIELD   "<C-struct-field>"]
                             [FUNCTION <change-func>]
                             [SPECIAL  <special-type>]*
                             [DBACCESS <group> <access>]*
                             [<specific-error-label>]
                     [,<attribute-label><propertylist>
                             [FIELD   "<C-struct-field>"]
                             [FUNCTION <change-func>]
```

```
                                          [SPECIAL   <special-type>]*
                                          [DBACCESS <group> <access>]*
                                          [<specific-error-label>]]* ;
                    ]
                    [GROUP ATTRIBUTES <group-label>[<attribute-label>]*
                                [,<group-label>[<attribute-label>]*]* ;
                    ]
                    [OPERATIONS
                            [PROVISION  [DBACCESS <group> [,<group>]*];
                            ]
                            [CREATE     [FUNCTION <create-func>]
                                        [DBACCESS <group> [,<group>]*];
                            ]
                            [DEFAULT CREATE FUNCTION <def-create-func>;
                            ]
                            [DELETE     <delete-modifier>
                                        [FUNCTION <create-func>]
                                        [DBACCESS <group> [,<group>]*];
                            ]
                            [ACTIONS <action-label>
                                        [<specific-error-label>]
                                    [,<action-label>
                                        [<specific-error-label>]]* ;
                            ]
                    ]
                    [NOTIFICATIONS <notification-label>
                                        [<specific-error-label>]
                                  [,<notification-label>
                                        [<specific-error-label>]]* ;
                    ]
                    [PACKAGE <package-label>
                                PRESENT IF <condition-definition> ;
                    ]*
                    [PROMPT "<user-friendly-prompt>" ;
                    ]
                    [IMAGES:
                            [CHILD  <image_label> ;]
                            [PARENT <image_label> ;]
                    ]
            ]
        [CONDITIONAL PACKAGES <package-label> PRESENT IF <condition>
                        [,<package-label> PRESENT IF <condition>]*;
        ]
        [PARAMETERS <parameter-label> [,parameter-label]* ;
        ]
REGISTERED AS <object-identifier> ;

supporting productions:
```

```
   propertylist ->     [GET | REPLACE | GET-REPLACE]

 delete-modifier ->   only-if-no-contained-object
                      | deletes-contained-objects

access ->            READ | WRITE | READWRITE

****************************************************************************
****************************************************************************
<attribute_label>    ATTRIBUTE
     [DERIVED FROM          <attribute-label> ;]
     [WITH ATTRIBUTE SYNTAX <syntax-label> ;]
     [MATCHES FOR           <qualifier>[,<qualifier>]* ;]
     [PERMITTED VALUES
            [RANGE          <low-number> TO <high-number>;
            ]
     ]
     [BEHAVIOR              <behavior-definition-label> ;]
     [DEFAULT               ["] <default-value> ["];]
     [PROMPT                "<user-friendly-prompt>" ;]
     [DBACCESS              <dbgroup><access>[,<dbgroup><access>]*;]
     [ANNOTATIONAL;]
REGISTERED AS <object-identifier> :

 syntax-label ->     INTEGER | OCTETSTRING | NetAddr | PrintableString

 qualifier -> Equality | Ordering | Substrings | Set Comparison
             | Set Intersection

 special-type -> OP_STATUS | ADMIN_STATUS | RDN
             | SERVICE_USER | SERVICE_PROVIDER

 access ->   READ | WRITE | READWRITE

****************************************************************************
****************************************************************************
 name definition (defines containment tree)
<name-binding-label> NAME BINDING
     SUBORDINATE OBJECT CLASS      <class-label>;
     NAMED BY
     SUPERIOR OBJECT CLASS         <class-label>;
            [WITHIN ANCHOR         <anchor-label>
                                        [,<anchor-label>]* ;]
     [WITH ATTRIBUTE               <attribute-label>;
     ]
 REGISTERED AS <object-identifier>;
****************************************************************************
****************************************************************************
<anchor_label>       ANCHOR POINT
```

```
                        X              Constant;
                        Y              Constant;
                        PROMPT         "<user-friendly-string>";
                        EMPTY IMAGE    <image_label>;

************************************************************************
************************************************************************
  <syntax-label> ::= SEQUENCE
        SPECIAL <special_identifier>
        {
        <name>  <syntax>
                [ DEFAULT      <default_value> ]
                [ PROMPT       "<display-str>" ]
                [ PERMITTED VALUES
                        [RANGE         <low-number> TO <high-number>
                        ]
                ] ;
        [ <name>       <syntax>
                [ DEFAULT      <default_value> ]
                [ PROMPT       "<display-str>" ]
                [ PERMITTED VALUES
                        [RANGE         <low-number> TO <high-number>
                        ]
                ] ;
        ]
  }


************************************************************************
************************************************************************
    <label>NOTIFICATION
        BEHAVIOUR <label> [, <label>]* ;
        MODE confirmation-mode;
        [ PARAMETERS <label> [, <label>]*;]
  [WITH INFORMATION SYNTAX <syntax-label>
   [AND ATTRIBUTE IDS <field-name> <attr-label>
                                        [FIELD "<C-struct>"]
                    [, <field-name> <attr-label>
                                        [FIELD "<C-struct>"]
                                                        ]* ;]
        [ WITH REPLY SYNTAX <syntax-label>; ]
  REGISTERED AS <object-identifier> ;

  confirmation-mode -> CONFIRMED | NON-CONFIRMED |
                    CONFIRMED AND NON-CONFIRMED


************************************************************************
************************************************************************
  <label> BEHAVIOUR
        DEFINED AS <text> ;
[REGISTERED AS <object-identifier>;]
```

```
*******************************************************************
*******************************************************************
<label> ATTRIBUTE GROUP
      [ GROUP ELEMENTS <label> [, <label>]* ; ]
      [ DESCRIPTION <descriptive-text> ]
REGISTERED AS <object-identifier>;


*******************************************************************
*******************************************************************
<action-label> ACTION
      [
      BEHAVIOUR <label> [, <label>]* ;
      ]
      [
      MODE confirmation-mode ;
      ]
      [PARAMETERS <label> [, <label>]*;]
      [WITH INFORMATION SYNTAX <label>;]
      [WITH REPLY SYNTAX <label>;]

REGISTERED AS <object-identifier> ;


*******************************************************************
*******************************************************************
<label> PARAMETER
      CONTEXT <context-type>;
      [ WITH SYNTAX <syntax-label> ; ]
      [ BEHAVIOUR <label> [, <label>]* ; ]
[ REGISTERED AS <object-identifier> ] ;

context-type -> ACTION-INFO | ACTION-REPLY | EVENT-INFO | EVENT-REPLY |
                SPECIFIC-ERROR | COMMON-ERROR | label
```

As mentioned earlier, this is an expanded template set and the developer should consult the template set that comes with their MIB compiler. Of course if you are not using a MIB compiler, you should stick with the very basic templates in the development of your MIB.

It should be observed that there are references to a database in the template above. Those references relate to the use of a conventional database. HP supports several databases. IBM and AT&T support only Ingress at this time. PEER and some of the agent packages also support databases of one kind or another.

Template Usage

There is good deal of confusion that comes from templates, their role, and how they are used. A TEMPLATE really is a guide nothing more, and nothing less. It instructs the user about what fields are available and what can be applied to the field. The TEMPLATE maps to a structure, the fields of which are filled by the information provided in the SMI encoding. Note that a number of vendors have expanded on this TEMPLATE, and those vendors require compliance with their TEMPLATE as well as with the Standard TEMPLATE.

The TEMPLATE forms the basis for a formal definition of whatever that TEMPLATE may relate to. There are a number of TEMPLATEs for example NOTIFICATION presented below. Some vendors expand their compilers to be able to deal with other templates. One of the best examples of this is the HP Metadata compiler. Their Metadata compiler is documented to "support any MIB definition (Internet)." Although the next line of the documentation states "the Metadata compiler has some specific rules and interpretations of the SMI."

From the HP TEMPLATE you may get a feeling of object orientation, and your feeling would be correct. The OpenView platform is object-oriented and supports such concepts as classes and inheritance.

How does the expanded HP TEMPLATE affect you? Well, in reality it doesn't—unless you are building a management application to run there. What it does do is point out that one of the biggest players in the network management area is not limited by Internet SMI rules but they are compatible with all the rules. There is a difference...

```
OBJECT-TYPE MACRO ::=
BEGIN
    TYPE NOTATION ::=
                    "SYNTAX" type(Syntax)
                    UnitsPart
                    "MAX-ACCESS" Access
                    "STATUS" Status
                    "DESCRIPTION" Text
                    ReferPart
                    IndexPart
                    DefValPart

    VALUE NOTATION ::=
                    value(VALUE ObjectName)

    UnitsPart ::=
                    "UNITS" Text
                  | empty
```

```
Access ::=
                "not-accessible"
              | "read-only"
              | "read-write"
              | "read-create"

Status ::=
                "current"
              | "deprecated"
              | "obsolete"

ReferPart ::=
                "REFERENCE" Text
              | empty

IndexPart ::=
                "INDEX"     "{" IndexTypes "}"
              | "AUGMENTS" "{" Entry         "}"
              | empty
IndexTypes ::=
                IndexType
              | IndexTypes "," IndexType

IndexType ::=
                "IMPLIED" Index
              | Index
Index ::=
                 — use the SYNTAX value of the
                 — correspondent OBJECT-TYPE invocation
                value(Indexobject ObjectName)
Entry ::=
                 — use the INDEX value of the
                 — correspondent OBJECT-TYPE invocation
                value(Entryobject ObjectName)

DefValPart ::=
                "DEFVAL" "{" value(Defval Syntax) "}"
              | empty

Text ::= """" string """"
END
```

It is important to look at what functionality is provided by the various fields. All of the fields are discussed in detail in the RFC, and only high points are presented here.

The ACCESS clause must be present, and it must provide the definition for the minimum support required by this object. Many MIB compilers will reject the field if an ACCESS is not defined for any OBJECT that has a read-write access.

The STATUS clause, which must be present, defines the implementation support required for that object type.

The DESCRIPTION clause need not be present, but when it is, it contains a textual definition of that object type which provides all semantic definitions necessary for implementation.

Note that, in order to conform to the ASN.1 syntax, the entire value of this clause must be enclosed in double quotation marks.

The REFERENCE clause, need not be present, contains a textual cross-reference.

The INDEX clause, which may be present only if that object type corresponds to a conceptual row, defines instance identification information for that object type.

The DEFVAL clause, need not be present but if used, it defines an acceptable default value that may be used with an object instance.

Notification

The Internet TEMPLATE for NOTIFICATION (TRAPS) is readily available through the Internet and RFCs. This template, as with all the others, is simply a guide to the format. There are hundreds of templates available through the Internet, some for SNMP, some for CMIP, and some for compilers that will process various combinations. Compatibility with the standards and usability by the compiler you use are the important factors to remember.

```
The NOTIFICATION TEMPLATE

    <label>   NOTIFICATION
            BEHAVIOR <label> [, <label>]* ;
            MODE confirmation-mode;
            [ PARAMETERS <label> [, <label>]*;]
      [WITH INFORMATION SYNTAX <syntax-label>
      [AND ATTRIBUTE IDS <field-name> <attr-label>
                    [, <field-name> <attr-label>
                                ]* ;]
            [ WITH REPLY SYNTAX <syntax-label>; ]
      REGISTERED AS <object-identifier> ;

      confirmation-mode -> CONFIRMED | NON-CONFIRMED |
                        CONFIRMED AND NON-CONFIRMED
```

USING SMI ENCODING

The SMI compiler input file (MIB) used to generate the "C" code, has the nature of many programming languages. For example, "ifdef" is used as in "C." Below we look at an example to depict the use of the templates covered earlier. It is important to understand that this file is the input to a compiler. Even when SMI code complies with the basic specifications it may not compile. Many compilers have their own quirks to contend with. Several MIB definitions are IMPORTed by this code. These IMPORTs provide a way for the compiler to resolve the various types.

```
#ifndef DDUCK_MIB_SMI
#define DDUCK_MIB_SMI

#include "snmptypes.h"
#include "dduck.h"

DDUCK-MIB DEFINITIONS ::= BEGIN

IMPORTS
        mgmt, NetworkAddress, IpAddress, Counter, Gauge, TimeTicks
                FROM RFC1442-SMI
        OBJECT-TYPE
                FROM RFC-1212:

NOTE: Basic SMI OBJECT IDENTIFIERS are left out for simplicity.

dduck4         OBJECT IDENTIFIER ::= { enterprises xyz }
systems        OBJECT IDENTIFIER ::= { dduck4 1 }

- The following variables are in the order required
- to support MIB II. The MIB II variables are then
- followed by the enterprises variables. The MIB
- could be separated to allow only the enterprise
- variables to be used.

- object types

- the System group
sysDescr OBJECT-TYPE
        SYNTAX  DisplayString (SIZE (0..255))
        ACCESS  read-only
        STATUS  mandatory
        DESCRIPTION
        "A textual description of the entity.  This value
        should include the full name and version
        identification of the system's hardware type,
        software operating-system, and networking
        software.  It is mandatory that this only contain
        printable ASCII characters."
        ::= { system 1 }
```

It is easy to see that the SMI/MIB is created using the various templates and laid out in a relational, ordered fashion.

(Lines which start with a dash (-) are comment lines.)

ENTERPRISE MIB CREATION

The purpose of creating your own MIB is to define your data. To do, that you will need to know about the elements that make up a MIB. We have already covered the creation of a standard MIB, the Enterprise MIB is an expansion of the same concepts. Through the study of this material, looking at existing MIBs and further study, you should be able to construct an intelligent MIB.

As the data related to the equipment is gathered, the vendor will come to the realization that there is a good deal of work both in the gathering and formulation of the data. The vendor should always be cautious in that the MIB can grow to be unmanageable very quickly. In the creation of the MIB, the vendor should consider what management of the equipment really means. For example, does managing the equipment include knowing what is in every register or about every insignificant variable?

The developer must also take into consideration the various quirks related to MIB compilers. The developer will want to concentrate on the MIB compiler it selects for use. Some of the commercial agents come with compilers, while the public domain agents generally do not. Although there is a general MIB compiler with ISODE that can be used, the developer should also compile the MIB using the commercial management compilers.

Publicly Available MIB Compilers (copyrighted)

- SMIC (SNMP MIB Compiler)
  Available at:
  Host: ftp.synoptics.com
  Area: /eng/mibcompiler

- MOSY (Managed Object Syntax-compiler Yacc-based)
  Available at:
  Host: ftp.uu.net
  Area: /networking/iso/isode

Commercial Compilers

- MIB 2 Schema (SunNet Manager)
  Sun Microsystems Corp.
  2550 Garcia Avenue
  Mountain View, CA 94043

- Open View Network Node Manager
  Hewlett-Packard Co.
  3404 E. Harmony Road
  Ft. Collins, CO 80525

- GDMOC
  PEER Networks, Inc.
  3375 Scott Boulevard
  Santa Clara, CA 95054

- Technology Conversion, Inc.
  3326 Transit Avenue
  Sioux City, IA 51106
  Ph: (712) 276-4024

This is not intended to be a complete list or a representation of quality.

FOR FURTHER STUDY

The following documents contain useful information that is beyond the scope of this chapter.

Perkins, David. *Understanding SNMP MIBs*, "White Paper." July 7, 1992.

Recommendation X.200, "Reference Model of Open Systems Interconnection for CCITT Applications." (See also ISO 7498.)

Recommendation X.208, Specification of Abstract Syntax Notation One (ASN.1) (See also ISO 8824.)

RSA PKCS #s (6-7-8-9) White papers relating to RSA Data Security, Inc. various parts of MIBs Redwood City, CA and encoding.

Extensible SNMP Agent Administrator's Reference, "Tech Manual." Hewlett-Packard Company, 3404 East Harmony Road, Fort Collins, CO 80525-9599.

REFERENCES

Galvin, J. and K. McCloghrie. *Security Protocols for version 2 of the Simple Network Management Protocol (SNMPv2)*, "RFC 1446." Internet request for comment. April 1993.

Galvin, J. and K. McCloghrie. *Party MIB for version 2 of the Simple Network Management Protocol*, "RFC 1447." Internet request for comment. April 1993.

7

Issues and Problems

INTRODUCTION

Given that SNMP was created to fill the gap until the OSI management protocols were completed, it has actually shown few problems. The public domain software from MIT and CMU has been ported to various platforms with few problems. A few problems do exist. Most of the real, significant problems, relate to the overall Internet mentality. That mentality evolves around the UNIX environment and the related network protocols, TCP/IP. With UNIX being a time sharing system and TCP/IP being the preferred networking the move to other architectures can be interesting. Many of the advances in technology, both hardware and software, have remedied some of the problems. For example Microsoft Windows and Windows NT lend themselves to SNMP nicely. Unfortunately, not to many companies want to have to run such a large operating system on an embedded system just to have SNMP.

Additionally, there is a movement among PC vendors to implement management standards that do not fit the SNMP mold. Companies working on DMI (Desktop Management Interface) have gone away from the SNMP trend. They have made accommodations for SNMP, but they are only accommodations and do not fit well or work well when interfaced to SNMP. The Desktop Management Task Force (DMTF) has chosen to try a different approach that will require a good deal of work before it is usable for a commercial environment.

Microsoft, a major industry force, seems to be leaning towards SNMP and away from DMTF, slowing the interest in DMTF.

THE MIB COMPILER

In the process of compiling an agent, there may be several compilers involved. The first compiler will generally be the hosts MIB compiler. In reality, the MIB compiler will utilize the first pass of the host compiler. This compiler processes the MIBs SMI coding into another programming language. That language will generally be "C" code. That code is then compiled along with the agent code. This step will utilize the target compiler, which in most cases will be a compiler targeted at an embedded system operating for a real time OS. Care must be exercised to assure that the compilers used are compatible with the target environment.

Since the MIB compiler uses the hosts own compiler, it is easy to generate structures that will not compile on the target system. The target systems compiler should be used to compile the MIB. This is done by setting the variable CC to the path of the target compiler, not the host compiler.

After the SMI encoding has been compiled and "C" code generated, the output will also contain function stubs that reflect the calls required by the variables. It must be noted that all MIB compilers do not generate these stubs. In some cases the access stubs will have to be generated by hand.

Not all agents expect MIB compiler output, nor will they utilize it. To make matters worse some agents do not work with the output off some compilers since there is no real standard in this area. This only becomes an issue in the cases in which a public domain or commercial agent/compiler is being used. If you are doing either part of the equation yourself, it is easy to adjust the input or output to accommodate the other.

Most commercial compilers provide the complete source code for the compiler. In the source code there is a number of output routines which can be tuned to the agent that is being used.

Below are examples of the output routines used by a standard GDMO compiler.

```
/* function to print NotifObj */
void
pNotifObj (FILE *stream, NotifObj *p, int32 ilev)
{
    ilev++;
    if (stream == NULL)
      stream = stdout;
    if (p) {
#ifdef PRINT_DOC_NAME
      if (p->documentName)
           fprintf(stream, "%s\tNOTIF DOC\n",p->documentName);
#endif
      if (p->templateName)
```

```
                    fprintf(stream, "%s\tNOTIFICATION\n",p->templateName);
        /* print behaviours */
        if (p->behaviours) {
                indent(stream, ilev);
                fprintf(stream, "BEHAVIOUR\t");
                pTemplateLabelList (stream, p->behaviours, ilev);
                fprintf(stream, ";\n");
}
/* print parameters */
if (p->parameters) {
        indent(stream, ilev);
        fprintf(stream, "PARAMETERS\t");
        pTemplateLabelList (stream, p->parameters, ilev);
}

/* print withInfoSyntax */
if ((p->withInfoSyntax) && (p->withInfoSyntax->T==presentTag)) {
        indent(stream, ilev);
        fprintf(stream, "WITH INFORMATION SYNTAX\t");
        pWithSyntax (stream, p->withInfoSyntax, ilev);
}

/* print andAttrIds */
if (p->andAttrIds) {
        indent(stream, ilev);
        fprintf(stream, "AND ATTRIBUTE IDS\n");
        pAndAttributeIds (stream, p->and AttrIds, ilev);
        fprintf(stream, ";\n");
} else
        fprintf(stream, ";\n");

/* print withReplySyntax */
if ((p->withReplySyntax) && (p->withReplySyntax->t==presentTag)) {
        indent(stream, ilev);
        fprint(stream, "WITH REPLY SYNTAX\t");
    fprintf(stream, "%s\tNOTIFICATION\n",p->templateName);

/* print behaviours */
if (p->behaviours) {
        indent(stream, ilev);
        fprintf(stream, "BEHAVIOUR\t");
        pTemplateLabelList (stream, p->behaviours, ilev);
        fprintf(stream, ";\n");
    if (stream == NULL)
         stream = stdout;

    if (p) {
#ifdef PRINT_DOC_NAME
        if (p->documentName)
            fprintf(stream, "%s\tNOTIF DOC\n",p->documentName);
#endif
```

```
if (p->templateName)
    fprintf(stream, "%s\tNOTIFICATION\n",p->templateName);

/* print behaviours */
if (p->behaviours) {
    indent(stream, ilev);
    fprintf(stream, "BEHAVIOUR\t");
    pTemplateLabelList (stream, p->behaviours, ilev);
    fprintf(stream, ";\n");
}
/* print parameters */
if (p->parameters) {
    indent(stream, ilev);
    fprintf(stream, "PARAMETERS\t");
    pTemplateLabelList (stream, p->parameters, ilev);
    fprintf(stream, ";\n");
}
/* print withInfoSyntax */
if ((p->withInfoSyntax) && (p->withInfoSyntax->t == presentTag)) {
    indent(stream, ilev);
    fprintf(stream, "WITH INFORMATION SYNTAX\t");
    pWithSyntax (stream, p->withInfoSyntax, ilev);
}

/* print andAttrIds */
if (p->andAttrIds) {
    indent(stream, ilev);
    fprintf(stream, "AND ATTRIBUTE IDS\n");
    pAndAttributeIds (stream, p->and AttrIds, ilev);
    fprintf(stream, ";\n");
} else
    fprintf(stream, ";\n");

/* print withReplySyntax */
if ((p->withReplySyntax) && (p->withReplySyntax->t == presentTag)) {
    indent(stream, ilev);
    fprintf(stream, "WITH REPLY SYNTAX\t");
    fprintf(stream, "%s\tNOTIFICATION\n",p->templateName);

/* print behaviours */
if (p->behaviours) {
    indent(stream, ilev);
    fprintf(stream, "BEHAVIOUR\t");
    pTemplateLabelList (stream, p->behaviours, ilev);
    fprintf(stream, ";\n");
}

/* print parameters */
if (p->parameters ) {
    indent(stream, ilev);
    fprintf(stream, "PARAMETERS\t");
    pTemplateLabelList (stream, p->parameters, ilev);
```

```
            fprintf(stream, ";\n");
    }

    /* print withInfoSyntax */
    if ((p->withInfoSyntax) && (p->withInfoSyntax->t == presentTag)) {
            indent(stream, ilev);
            fprintf(stream, "WITH INFORMATION SYNTAX\t");
            pWithSyntax (stream, p->withInfoSyntax, ilev);
    }

    /* print andAttrIds */
    if (p->andAttrIds) {
            indent(stream, ilev);
            fprintf(stream, "AND ATTRIBUTE IDS\n");
            pAndAttributeIds (stream, p->andAttrIds, ilev);
            fprintf(stream, ";\n");
    } else
            fprintf(stream, ";\n");

    /* print withReplySyntax */
    if ((p->withReplySyntax) && (p->withReplySyntax->t == presentTag)) {
            indent(stream, ilev);
            fprintf(stream, "WITH REPLY SYNTAX\t");
            pWithSyntax (stream, p->withReplySyntax, ilev);
            fprintf(stream, ";\n");
    }

    /* print registeredAs */
    if (p->registeredAs) {
            indent(stream, ilev-1); /* indent (ilev); */
            fprintf(stream, "REGISTERED AS { ");
            pRegisteredAs (stream, p->registeredAs, ilev);
            fprintf(stream, ");\n");
    }
  }
}


/* function to print ActionObj */
voic
pActionObj (FILE *stream, ActionObj *p, int32 ilev)
{
  ilev++;

  if (stream == NULL)
      stream = stdout;
    if(p->documentName)
        fprintf(stream, "%s\tACTION DOC\n", p->documentName);
```

```
#endif
    /* print templateName */
    if (p->templateName)
        fprintf(stream, "%s\t ACTION\n", p->templateName);

    /* print behaviours */
    if (p->behaviours) {
        indent(stream, ilev);
        fprintf(stream, "BEHAVIOUR\t");
        pTemplateLabelList (stream, p->behaviours, ilev);
     fprintf(stream, ";\n");
    }
    /* print modeConfirmed */
    if (p->modeConfirmed) {
        indent(stream, ilev);
        fprintf(stream, "MODE\tCONFIRMED;\n");
    }
    /* print parameters */
    if (p->parameters) {
        indent(stream, ilev);
        fprintf(stream, "PARAMETERS\t");
        pTemplateLabelList (stream, p->parameters, ilev);
        fprintf(stream, ";\n");
    }

    /* print withInfoSyntax */
    if ((p->withInfoSyntax) && (p->withInfoSyntax->t == presentTag)) {
        indent(stream, ilev);
        fprintf(stream, "WITH INFORMATION SYNTAX\t");
        pWithSyntax (stream, p->withInfoSyntax, ilev);
        fprintf(stream, ";\n");
    }
    /* print withgReplySyntax */
    if ((p->withReplySyntax) && (p->withReplySyntax->t == presentTag)) {
        indent(stream, ilev);
        fprintf(stream, "WITH REPLY SYNTAX\t");
        pWithSyntax (stream, p->withReplySyntax, ilev);
        fprintf(stream, ";\n");
    }

    /* print registeredAs */
    if (p->registeredAs) {
        indent(stream, ilev-I); /* indent (ilev); */
        fprintf(stream, "REGISTERED AS\t{ ");
        pRegisteredAs (stream, p->registeredAs, ilev);
        fprintf(stream, " };\n");
    }
}
```

Some of the do-it-yourself agents can take their own form of input, making a MIB compiler worthless. Some agents actually read up the MIB at run time. It has been suggested that this makes them more flexible. That is not necessarily true; some agents, as well as management systems, can read and use the SMI file as input and compile and link at run time. Still other agents utilize MIB libraries via a UNIX concept of shared libraries. Most real time OSs running on embedded systems can better utilize compiler output that can be compiled into their source. The other concepts are somewhat out of place on most embedded systems since most don't have file systems. Therefore, they can not utilize a shared library, and they have no need to bind to a new MIB at runtime.

Various compilers have differing output, but it must be clear that the compiler output is very important to the overall implementation. Compiler output has been presented elsewhere and will not be presented again here. A good deal of work is involved even after the compiler is done. For example, many stub functions are generated that must be filled in by the implementors. The compiler output can in some cases become overbearing. When compiled, some MIBs will exceed 9,000 lines with over 600 function stubs. That was just the private MIB portion, the complete MIB can be much larger. When a number of MIBs are coupled together on a management station, the MIB grew to well over 25,000 lines (several megabytes). Most of the lines are structures and other such elements that are not a great deal of trouble for the implementors. However, the volume alone can become troublesome when limited memory is available. It should also be considered that the MIB will be placed with your clients, and they will need to compile the MIB into their management station. A huge MIB may be more than any client wants to bear, or worse, their system may not be able to handle it because of memory limitations.

It must be understood that no matter how the MIB is done, with a compiler or by hand, the access routines must be developed. The MIB compiler can ease some of the burden, but nothing will relieve the developer of that task. The task of developing these routines can become very large, depending upon the size of the MIB.

Anyone implementing SNMP should be cautious of MIB compilers that utilize proprietary formats, although a proprietary compiler is better than the brute force, hard-code-it-in approach. Any compiler will give some assurance of portability. It will also help you to find problems before the end user.

It has been stated that brute force coding of the agent code is the best approach. Personally, if I have tools that will ease my life, I use them. In these days where time to market is tight and all of us are being overloaded, I would be hard pressed to believe that the cost of a compiler could not be justified. I cannot believe that the code could be that much tighter or better when done by hand. I would believe that with the new processors running at 60 or more MHz and doing multiple instruction per clock cycle, we would have difficulty making a case that a few lines of code could matter. Yes, I know there will be those who say that a few lines of code can kill you, but in reality, if your code is that bad, or your project is that tight, this book probably is not the answer to your problem.

COMPILER OUTPUT

Although the MIB may have run through the compiler it is not necessarily correct. Even worse, it may not run through the compiler. Some times the base problem will be complex, while other times, it will be a simple issue of compiler quirks and every compiler has at least one. The real key to a quality compiler is that they comply with the GDMO standard. Unfortunately, even the compilers that do comply with the GDMO standard can operate differently, since the standard leaves room for interpretation.

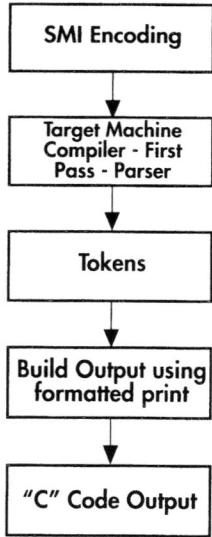

Figure 7.1 Compiler Operation.

Many compilers offer lists of options such as the ability to count the objects in the MIB. Some have options to create skeletons and various other types of output. The single most important output is the creation of procedure skeletons, and this should be a requirement of whatever compiler is used.

Another valuable characteristic of some compilers is the ability to list important statistics about the MIB. These statistics can include the number of

Traps, the total imports, the total exports, etc. Not all compilers will generate such detail, but it is clearly an advantage if they do, since the implementation of the MIB can be difficult.

INTERFACE ERRORS

Since the MIB interface really is responsible for the values contained in the variables, the interface logic, the stubs, and the related code must be correct. Yet in all too many cases it is not. This is best depicted by the fact that in a study done by a trade journal most agents did not return correct values. Some were off by rather large amounts in some very basic areas. Unfortunately, the agent was blamed for the problems when in most cases the problem was probably with the MIB or the ACCESS stubs. Other issues, such as what is a packet, also come into play. At first glance one would say a packet is a packet is a packet. But what about the case in which a number of fragments are sent, and some are dropped and retransmitted and dropped again and once again retransmitted. Which part of that constitutes a packet, and how is it calculated? What if the network is 100% busy, and 60% of it is retransmissions? How is that represented to the network manager?

Some agents actually returned 0 (zero) for a number of the variables they claim to support. This in fact, is probably due to a lack of interface logic or worse yet the implementor believed that the variable would somehow just get filled in by magic. Many times it ends up being a variable that did not get an access routine coded correctly.

OPERATING SYSTEM ISSUES

SNMP was originally targeted at the UNIX environment. This may have not been done intentionally, but the intent was for a time sharing system. In the MS-DOS (Microsoft Disk Operating System) used on most PCs there is no easy way to time slice between applications. That is the primary reason that most of the network management work is done under MS Windows. Windows provides the time slice capability so the networking application need not. This does not mean that SNMP cannot be done under DOS, but it does mean it will take more work. There are a number of methods by which SNMP can be made to work with DOS. It is not clear that one has an advantage over the other, but one of the best ways to do it is through the use of the MIT IP stack. This source code is available from MIT and other locations. It provides a time share system for a DOS environment. The code is mature and stable. It is so mature that references to the original PC can be found. By using the tasking functionality, all of the same capabilities of a time share system can be obtained.

Another approach to the PC environment is to use one of the public domain IP stacks that have capability of being interrupt driven. Then the whole process can be embedded within the application. However, this creates other issues that need to be dealt with, such as re-entrancy problems.

One other issue that plagues the PC environment is the overall architecture. The overwhelming power of the CPU chips leads many to believe that they can handle whatever comes their way, but this is not the case. The processor may be able to handle the work load, but the architecture will tend to become I/O bound in many instances. This is not completely the fault of the architecture and more an issue of the various vendors implementations of I/O cards and the never ending quest to keep the price down.

CONFIGURATION

SNMP utilizes the support of the network that it lives on. For example, SNMP will use the routing capabilities of the network. The network configuration must be set up correctly. The protocol stack must be able to get the data to SNMP. This may include handling fragments and other issues relating to networks. The configuration may be required to provide some basic parameters for SNMP as well. For example if the management station routes are kept in the MIB, with the MIB being dynamic, it will need to gather this information from some configuration file somewhere.

MEMORY ISSUES

With many SNMP agents the old line of "memory is cheap, just use more" is not always true. Many embedded systems do not have any additional memory available. In some cases memory is available, but the size of the MIB may over run what ever memory is available. In either of these cases, there is not a great deal that can be done. The best approach that has been found up to now is to utilize a conservative agent and MIB. The agent contained on the diskettes is the base code used by many vendors such as HP, IBM, and AT&T. It is a relatively small agent, and with a reasonably sized MIB, the size of the agent can be kept to under 40K. Other reductions can be made in the overall size by utilizing the right compiler, stripping the code at compile time, and using other tricks known to most code developers.

PORTABILITY ISSUES

There are a number of areas in which any of the agents can have problems when porting. Whether it is a commercial agent or a public domain version, the code can cause problems in areas, such as the ASN.1 ENCODING routines and the header files. In some cases, the ENCODE and DECODE routines will not assign types or sizes correctly. Some of the agents come with their own header files to try to assure portability. Unfortunately, the use of their own header files can create other issues when there are conflicts between headers that are included from some other file. The whole issue requires some additional work in most cases. Often the protocol structures defined in the headers will not match, creating even more problems. There can be issues of incompatible port and socket structures, primarily in the address fields. Some agents still use the old style Internet addressing while the system may use the newer addressing. In all cases the include files should be checked and double checked. Developers should also work to assure that when cross compiling code for another machine, the correct headers are included and not the host system headers. Often, the environment may be set up such that the path of the local includes will be used when there is an include nested in another include. Developers will some times hard code the source code and then the nested includes will still grab the wrong include. When this happens without the developer being aware of it, the outcome can be code that will execute somewhat and take forever to debug.

Most of these issues are known to all developers, but they are often overlooked. If you build either a commercial or public domain agent, you will more likely encounter these types of problems.

FOR FURTHER STUDY

The following documents contain useful information that is beyond the scope of this chapter.

Case, Jeff. *RFC1157*. (A Simple Network Management Protocol.)

Krol, Ed. *The Whole Internet User's Guide and Catalog.* ISBN 1-56592-025-2. November 1992. (Informative—relating to Internet access and usage.)

McCloghrie, K. and M.T. Rose. *RFC1155*. (Structure and Identification of Management Information for TCP/IP-based Internets.)

HP OpenView SNMP Agent Administrator's Guide. Hewlett-Packard, 3404 East Harmony Road, Fort Collins, CO 80525. (Good general information.)

8

TRAPs

INTRODUCTION

Many of the writings on SNMP have not emphasized TRAPs and their usage. I find that surprising, given the importance of letting the management station know what is taking place on the managed equipment. I have also seen clients get excessively excited about traps. One client spent over a million dollars to have the Icon flash red when a trap arrived. The icon would change colors, but not flash and to the client it was worth the money to assure that the icon flashed to draw the attention of the person monitoring the network.

Experiences with clients that made me aware of what importance TRAPs really had to the end user. Unfortunately TRAPs leave much to be desired for providing the support that most end users desire. For example, what happens to a trap when a system is already in trouble? If the managed equipment is dropping packets because the interface cannot handle the load, does the TRAP ever get out? If trap does get out, has the agent been constructed with some type of threshold so that a flood of TRAPs does not merely add to the already overloaded network? The issues relating to traps can go on and on. Some say that the logic of what happens with the TRAP is outside the scope of the SNMP agent, while others say TRAPs are the agents' responsibility. No matter which way it is viewed, it will not matter if the overall mechanism does not work.

In this chapter I address only the protocol of the trap. The actual implementation will take a good deal of thinking about the specifics of the system being developed. As an SNMP development takes place, the developer must keep the trap-directed polling approach of SNMP in mind. That approach, being a compromise between polling and the interrupt-driven mentality, requires a good deal of architecting in advance. Architecting is what we used to do before we had tight time-to-market developments.

PURPOSE

The purpose of the TRAP mechanism is very clear. It is to notify the management station of some event that has taken place that probably was not intended. That event can be something fairly simple, or it can be a major catastrophe. I have seen a number of examples here and there that use "myLinkDown" as a trap. I have always wondered how that trap got to the management platform if it was in-band service...just a thought.

Version	Community	Trap PDU

Figure 8.1 SNMP V1 TRAP.

The SNMPv1 TRAP was a separate form of PDU, while in V2 it has been modified to be consistent with other PDUs. This allows Manager-to-Manger communications. In V2 the capability for "InformRequest," manager-to-manager communication exists. This change has made the SNMPv1 obsolete in a V2 environment. Therefore, a developer must define the intended version early on. The V2 Trap is controlled by the access control list (ACL). This mechanism is defined in the Party MIB. This mechanism can be used to control what entity the TRAP is addressed to.

NOTE: The included source code (MIT version) has the ACL mechanics in place. This makes it an excellent study vehicle for development of the Party MIB.

USAGE

Enterprise-specific Trap

Consider a simple example of an enterprise-specific trap that is sent when a communication link failure is encountered:

```
myEnterprise OBJECT IDENTIFIER ::= { enterprises 9999 }

myLinkDown TRAP-TYPE
    ENTERPRISE  myEnterprise
    VARIABLES   { ifIndex }
    DESCRIPTION
              "A myLinkDown trap signifies that the sending
              SNMP application entity recognizes a failure in
```

```
                           one of the communications links represented
                           in the agent's configuration."
              ::= 6
```

CONSTRUCTS

The TRAP mechanism, initially defined in the RFC 1215, is outlined below.

```
<trap-name>           TYPE TYPE
      ENTERPRISE      <object-identifier>)
      [VARIABLES      {<snmp-var> [, <snmp-var>] *}]
      [DESCRIPTION    "<description>"]
      [REFERENCE      "<reference-text>"]
      ::= <trap-number>
```

An example of the usage of a trap:

```
overTemp      TRAP-TYPR
              ENTERPRISE        thisEnterprise
              VARIABLES         { ifIndex }
              DESCRIPTION       " The box is over temperature. Please
                                consult the temperature variable to
                                determine the current temperature."
              ::= 9
```

The exact **TRAP-TYPE** macro could use a bit more explanation, which follows.

```
TRAP-TYPE MACRO ::=
BEGIN
    TYPE NOTATION ::= "ENTERPRISE" value
              (enterprise OBJECT IDENTIFIER)
            VarPart
            DescrPart
            ReferPart
    VALUE NOTATION ::= value (VALUE INTEGER)

    VarPart ::=
        "VARIABLES" "{" VarTypes "}"
          | empty
    VarTypes ::=
        VarType | VarTypes "," VarType
    VarType ::=
        value (vartype ObjectName)

    DescrPart ::=
        "DESCRIPTION" value (description DisplayString)
          | empty
```

```
ReferPart ::=
       "REFERENCE" value (reference DisplayString)
        | empty

END
```

V2 Traps

If a Trap-PDU is received, it is mapped into a SNMPv2-Trap-PDU. This is done by prepending onto the variable-bindings field two new bindings: sysUpTime.0, which takes its value from the timestamp field of the Trap-PDU; and snmpTrapOID.0, which is calculated thus: if the value of generic-trap field is 'enterpriseSpecificc,' then the value used is the concatenation of the enterprise field from the Trap-PDU with two additional sub-identifiers, '0,' and the value of the specific-trap field; otherwise, the value of the corresponding trap defined is used. (For example, if the value of the generic-trap field is 'coldStart,' then the coldStart trap is used.) Then, one new binding is appended onto the variable-binding's field: snmpTrapEnterpriseOID.0, which takes its value from the enterprise field of the Trap-PDU.

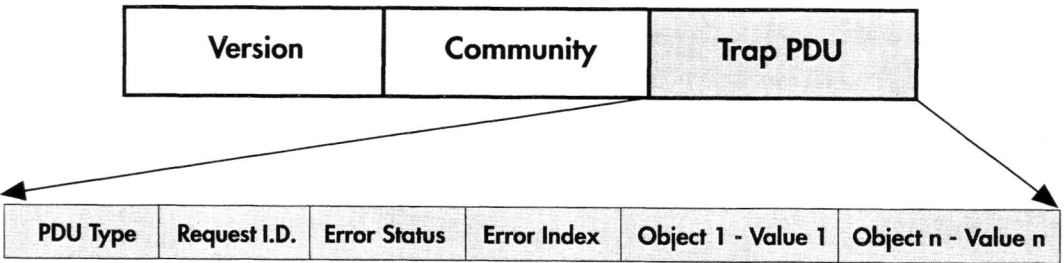

Figure 8.2 TRAP Message.

The TRAP PDU

The format for a TRAP PDU takes the form:

Enterprise field—which identifies the type of equipment generating the trap.

Agent address—is the address of the equipment generating the trap.

Trap type field—which tells the nature of the event.

Time Stamp—tells when the trap was generated.

Variable bindings—provides useful information that was selected via the MIB implementation.

The TRAP PDU format within an IP packet format is presented below.

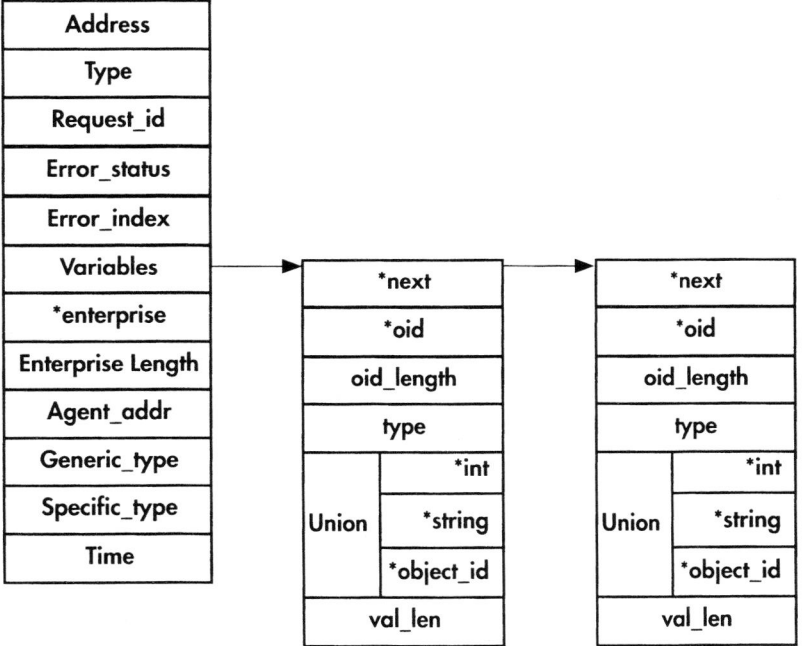

Figure 8.3 SNMP TRAP PDU.

* Also identifies duplicate traps.

STANDARD TRAPS

It was viewed that keeping the number of standard traps to a minimum was important. Therefore only six standard traps have been incorporated into the RFCs. They are:

```
coldStart TRAP-TYPE
    ENTERPRISE  snmp
    DESCRIPTION
            "A coldStart trap signifies that the sending
            protocol entity is reinitializing itself such
            that the agent's configuration or the protocol
            entity implementation may be altered."
```

```
                    ::= 0

warmStart TRAP-TYPE
    ENTERPRISE  snmp
    DESCRIPTION
                "A warmStart trap signifies that the sending
                protocol entity is reinitializing itself such
                that neither the agent configuration nor the
                protocol entity implementation is altered."
    ::= 1

linkDown TRAP-TYPE
    ENTERPRISE  snmp
    VARIABLES   { ifIndex }
    DESCRIPTION
                "A linkDown trap signifies that the sending
                protocol entity recognizes a failure in one of
                the communication links represented in the
                agent's configuration."
    ::= 2

linkUp TRAP-TYPE
    ENTERPRISE  snmp
    VARIABLES   { ifIndex }
    DESCRIPTION
                "A linkUp trap signifies that the sending
                protocol entity recognizes that one of the
                communication links represented in the agent's
                configuration has come up."
    ::= 3

authenticationFailure TRAP-TYPE
    ENTERPRISE  snmp
    DESCRIPTION
                "An authenticationFailure trap signifies that
                the sending protocol entity is the addressee
                of a protocol message that is not properly
                authenticated.  While implementations of the
                SNMP must be capable of generating this trap,
                they must also be capable of suppressing the
                emission of such traps via an implementation-
                specific mechanism."
    ::= 4

egpNeighborLoss TRAP-TYPE
    ENTERPRISE  snmp
    VARIABLES   { egpNeighAddr }
    DESCRIPTION
                "An egpNeighborLoss trap signifies that an EGP
                neighbor for whom the sending protocol entity
                was an EGP peer has been marked down and the
                peer relationship no longer obtains."
    ::= 5
```

The traps themselves are fairly explanatory, so I will only make a few small points about them. One is that the numbering sequence starts at 0 (zero) ending at 5, with enterprise specific traps starting at 6 and going up. The second point is the fact that a minimum number of defined traps was probably a wise direction since they can become dated. Consider, example "egpNeighborLoss." How many pieces of network equipment really utilize this trap?

MISCELLANEOUS

Traps seem to create more than their fair share of confusion for many developers. For reasons that are not clear to me, traps are often viewed as something that needs to be dealt with in some special manner. Traps are as any other element of the MIB, although there is a special arrangement for sending a trap PDU. Only some of the better developers will include information in the MIB that can be used to determine what traps are sent to what managers. All of this can easily be built into a table.

Another issue that seems to confuse many developers is the question of how to send a trap. There are many different methods used for the various agents but in most implementations the developer will find a "RAW" mode and a "COOKED" mode. The RAW mode will allow code to develop an SNMP trap and use the transport in a "RAW" mode to send the PDU. That is a very crude way and should probably be avoided if possible. The better choice is to utilize the internal functionality to build the PDU, the "COOKED" mode. In the example MIT code included on the diskettes, a programmer would need only call the functional trapCreate() to create the PDU and send it. The parameters used with the function call provide all the required information for the trap message to be created and sent. Most reasonable agents will have an interface that allows the trap to be created and sent without a great deal of additional work.

Another problem that seems to arise with traps is the question of "how does SNMP know to send a trap?" The answer is simply, SNMP does not know when. Your code must call the appropriate trap functionality at the appropriate time. For example, if you were building a network hub, every time there was an error condition that the network manager should know about, you would call the functionality to send a trap. That could require a lot of calls to be added to existing systems if a centralized error messaging approach was not implemented during the original design.

The developer will usually not realize all of the times that a trap must be sent from the agent. For example, the "Cold Start" trap is often overlooked. This trap should be sent as soon as the agent is started, yet caution must be used to assure that the MIB is loaded and available, or that any other initialization that may be required has been started. Many agents that are licensed and have an internal way to check the license will do so before they send a cold start trap. This approach is used so that the management station does not get notification from an agent that will exit because of an invalid license.

The addition of trap logic can be one place that requires a great deal of time for people adding SNMP to an existing system. Much thought should be given to exactly how this will be approached before the development begins.

An example of using the MIB/SMI to handle the TRAP information is presented below. It is lengthy to allow the required detail, yet it is far from complete, a creative developer could enhance it a great deal. Yet it provides some interesting ideas for those creating their first MIB.

```
xyzSpecificAlarmState OBJECT-TYPE
  SYNTAX INTEGER {
    disarmed(1),
    armed(2)
  }
  ACCESS read-write
  STATUS mandatory
  DESCRIPTION
    "This indicates whether the repeater is allowed to send specific
     alerts (traps). 1 means disabled, 2 means enabled to send alerts."
  ::= {xyzSpecificGroup 3}

xyzSpecificTrapDestEntry OBJECT-TYPE
  SYNTAX    XyzSpecificTrapDestEntry
  ACCESS    not-accessible
  STATUS    mandatory
  DESCRIPTION
        "Status information and control variables for a
         particular repeater in the system."
  INDEX    { xyzSpecificTrapId }
  ::= { xyzSpecificTrapDestTable 1 }

XyzSpecificTrapDestEntry ::= SEQUENCE {
  xyzSpecificTrapId              INTEGER,
  xyzSpecificTrapDstAdr  IpAddress,
  xyzSpecificTrapDstPro  INTEGER
}

xyzSpecificTrapId OBJECT-TYPE
  SYNTAX    INTEGER (1..127)
  ACCESS    read-only
  STATUS    mandatory
  DESCRIPTION
    "Number of Trap Destination entry. 1 for first entry, 2 for second
     entry, etc."
  ::= { xyzSpecificTrapDestEntry 1 }
```

```
xyzSpecificTrapDstAdr OBJECT-TYPE
  SYNTAX      IpAddress
  ACCESS      read-write
  STATUS      mandatory
  DESCRIPTION
  "This is an IP address to which alerts (traps) should be sent when
  significant events occur."
   ::= { xyzSpecificTrapDestEntry 2 }
xyzSpecificTrapDstPro OBJECT-TYPE
  SYNTAX      INTEGER {
    none(1),       — Disabled
    ip(2),         — TCP/IP
    ipxII(3),      — IPX Ethernet II
    ipx8022(4),     — IPX 802.2 RAW
    ipx8022SNAP(5), — IPX 802.2 SNAP
    ipx8023(6)     — IPX 802.3 Physical Layer
  }
  ACCESS      read-write
  STATUS      mandatory
  DESCRIPTION
    "This is a code indicating the protocol to use when sending alerts.
    1 means disabled, i.e. the corresponding xyzSpecificTrapDstAdr
    variable is not really intended to receive traps.  2 = TCP/IP protocol,
    3 = IPX protocol using Ethernet II, 4 = IPX protocol using RAW 802.2,
    5 = IPX protocol using 802.2 SNAP, 6 = IPX protocol using 802.3 physical
                                    layer."
   ::= { xyzSpecificTrapDestEntry 3 }


— Traps for use by Repeaters

— Traps are defined using the conventions in RFC 1215 [10].
  XyzExtPortEntry ::= SEQUENCE {
    xyzBasPortRptrId                    INTEGER,
    xyzBasPortGroupId                        INTEGER,
    xyzBasPortId                        INTEGER,
    xyzBasPortAdminState                INTEGER,
    xyzBasPortAutoPartitionState        INTEGER,
    xyzBasPortLinkState                 INTEGER,
    xyzAddrLastSourceAddress            MacAddress,
    xyzAddrSourceAddrChanges            Counter,
    xyzMonPortReadableFrames               Counter,
    xyzMonPortReadableOctets               Counter,
    xyzMonPortFrameCheckSequenceErrs       Counter,
    xyzMonPortAlignmentErrors              Counter,
    xyzMonPortFrameTooLongs                Counter,
    xyzMonPortShortEvents                  Counter,
    xyzMonPortRunts                        Counter,
    xyzMonPortCollisions                   Counter,
    xyzMonPortLateCollisions               Counter,
    xyzMonPortDataRateMismatches           Counter,
    xyzMonPortAutoPartitions               Counter
```

```
        }


    xyzDosWsTrapId OBJECT-TYPE
        SYNTAX    INTEGER (1..127)
        ACCESS    read-only
        STATUS    mandatory
        DESCRIPTION
        "Number of Trap Destination entry. 1 for first entry, 2 for second
        entry, etc."
        ::= { xyzDosWsTrapDestEntry 1 }

    xyzDosWsTrapDstAdr OBJECT-TYPE
        SYNTAX    IpAddress
        ACCESS    read-write
        STATUS    mandatory
        DESCRIPTION
        "This is an IP address to which alerts (traps) should be sent when
        significant events occur."
        ::= { xyzDosWsTrapDestEntry 2 }

    xyzDosWsTrapDstPro OBJECT-TYPE
        SYNTAX    INTEGER
        ACCESS    read-write
        STATUS    mandatory
        DESCRIPTION
        "This is a code indicating the protocol to use when sending alerts.
        1 means disabled, i.e. the corresponding xyzDosWsTrapDstAdr
        variable is not really intended to receive traps.  2 means use
        TCP/IP protocol.  3,4,5,6 mean use IPX protocol using Ethernet II,
        RAW 802.2, 802.2 SNAP or 802.3 physical layer."
        ::= { xyzDosWsTrapDestEntry 3 }

  xyzDosWsApiTrap OBJECT-TYPE
        SYNTAX    DisplayString
        ACCESS    read-only
        STATUS    mandatory
        DESCRIPTION
        "This is a string set by external applications
        which use the PC Agent API to send an SNMP trap "

        ::= { xyzDosWs 24 }

  xyzDiscover OBJECT-TYPE
        SYNTAX    INTEGER
        ACCESS    read-only
        STATUS    mandatory
        DESCRIPTION
        "This is used in agent discovery by EliteView "

        ::= { xyz 127 }
END
```

FOR FURTHER STUDY

The following documents contain useful information that is beyond the scope of this chapter.

RFC 1052, NRI. Cerf, V., "IAB Recommendations for the Development of Internet Network Management Standards." April 1988.

Rose, M. and K. McCloghrie. *RFC 1065, TWG* "Structure and Identification of Management Information, for TCP/IP-based internets." August 1988.

REFERENCES

Rose, M. *A Request for Comments: 1215.* "Convention for Defining Traps for use with the SNMP." March, 1991.

9

SNMP Commands

OVERVIEW

The SNMP command set is well-known, and readers may wonder why devote a chapter to the commands. I would suggest that it is important to take at least a small look at each command with comment as to their usage and error conditions.

As we look at the SNMP command set, it is important to realize that most will not see the command set directly. On the accompanying diskettes, there is a set of SNMP commands for testing and that may be the only time you will see them. The norm is to have a management station that translates higher level abstracts to the lower level GET/SET scenario, and by doing so, they often hide small issues that one needs to understand. To be able to understand those issues, the GET/SET commands must be understood.

An example of why such understanding may be important here. Let's say that a management station sends and SNMP GET Request to an agent. Suppose the packet is delayed on its arrival at the agent. During that time the management station, not getting a response, sends another GET and then receives the response from the first. In the meantime, the second GET response is dropped on the network. What does the NMS know at that time? Is the first GET used, or is another GET issued because a response from the second did not arrive?

NOTE: Only some management stations will generate another GET if the response is not forthcoming. Those that do generally have a time-out value that can be set for networks with slow response times.

To aid understanding Table 9.1 presents the command set for both V1 and V2.

COMMAND	DESCRIPTION	FROM - TO	V1	V2
Set	Assigns a value to a variable	NMS to Agent	YES	YES
Get	Returns value of variable(s)	NMS to Agent	YES	YES
GetNext	Returns value of list of variables	NMS to Agent	YES	YES
GetBulk	Returns a number of variables	NMS to Agent	NO	YES
Inform	Transmits unsolicited information	NMS to NMS	NO	YES
TRAP	Transmits unsolicited information	Agent to NMS	YES	YES
Responses	Responses to commands	Agent to NMS	YES	YES

Table 9.1 Command Set Comparison.

SNMP GET

The SNMP GET Command initiates a network management query to remote agent and causes a response to be transmitted by the agent. The SNMP GET command attempts to retrieve the items of management information.

From Manager - to Agent

PDU Type 0	Request I.D.	Error Status	Error Index	Object 1 - Value NULL	Object n - Value NULL

From Agent - to Manager

PDU Type 2	Request I.D.	Error Status	Error Index	Object 1 - Value 1	Object n - Value n

Figure 9.1 SNMP GET Request / Response.

The GET request can generate a number of errors that are returned from the agent. Those errors include noSuchName, tooBig, and genErr. The small set is expanded through the use of error index numbering. The common errors that arise from the agent are presented below.

- **Aggregate error**—this error arises when the management station has mistakenly tried to retrieve a row object. The error returned is "noSuchName" with an error index that indicates the variable.

- **Variable error**—this error is an indication of an attempt to retrieve a variable that cannot be retrieved. The error returned is "genErr" with the error index set.

- **Set error**—this error indicates that the response PDU would exceed some limitation known to the agent. The error returned is "tooBig" with the error index set.

- **Binding error**—this error is returned when a variable does not exactly match. The returned error is "noSuchName" with the appropriate index.

The error status/return has received a good deal of comment. It has been stated that they are not as clear as they could be. Also there is the thinking that someone trying to get information can extract some information, given the SNMP error returned. Both of these issues still receive a good deal of debate within the community.

SNMP GETNEXT

The SNMP GETNEXT command attempts to retrieve the specified subtrees of the MIB. The approach to the SNMP GETNEXT command may vary from agent to agent and NMS to NMS. The GETNEXT command can do what is called "run off." Run off is a condition in which the agent will pass or stick at the end of a table causing masses of worthless data. This behavior can be seen in the MIT agent included in the sample code. When a getnext is done on the route table the agent will often return routes infinitely.

From Manager - to Agent

PDU Type 1	Request I.D.	Error Status	Error Index	Object 1 - NULL	Object n - NULL

From Agent - to Manager

PDU Type 2	Request I.D.	Error Status	Error Index	Object 1 - Value 1	Object n - Value n

Figure 9.2 SNMP GETNEXT Request / Response.

The GETNEXT request can generate a number of errors that are returned from the agent. Those errors are the same as those from SNMP GET with slightly different causes. The set is expanded through the use of error index numbering. The common errors that arise from the agent are presented below.

- **Size error**—this error indicates that the response PDU would exceed some limitation known to the agent. The error returned is "tooBig" with the error index set.

- **Binding error**—this error is returned when a variable does not exactly match. The returned error is noSuchName with the appropriate index.

- **Lexicographical error**—this condition arises when the successor to a requested variable in the binding field can not be retrieved. The error status returned is genErr with the appropriate index.

The fact that many GETNEXT Implementations are lacking became apparent with the introduction of GETBULK. In particular, when a get-next request contains an operand with an arbitrarily generated suffix, some agent implementations will handle this improperly and return a result that is lexicographically less than the operand!

(In most agents getnext and getbulk use the same logic.)

SNMP GETBULK

The management station can repeatedly invoke the get-next operator, using the results of the previous operation as the operands to the next operation. This approach can be laborious. The approach of SNMP GETBULK was developed to alleviate the burden of repeated GETNEXT commands. GETBULK has a complete RFC dedicated to its implementation (RFC 1187). Although the RFC has been around for some time, there has not been a great deal of interest in GETBULK.

From Manager - to Agent

PDU Type 4	Request I.D.	Error Status	Error Index	Object n - Number

From Agent - to Manager

PDU Type 2	Request I.D.	Error Status	Error Index	Object 1 - Value 1	Object n - Value n

Figure 9.3 SNMP GETBULK Request / Response.

GETBULK returns the same types of errors as GETNEXT.

The GetBulkRequest operates essentially by executing multiple GetNext requests. The GetBulkRequest PDU is similar to other PDUs, except that the syntax of two fields changes. The fields Error Status is replaced by Non-Repeaters, and Error Index is replaced by Max-Repetitions. The values of these fields indicate the processing that is to take place. The Non-Repeaters field defines how many of the requested variables will not be processed repeatedly. This field is used when some of the variables are scalar objects, that is, objects having one instance.

The retrieved variables are returned in a Response PDU, according to the manner in which those variables were requested. The total number of variables can be calculated by:

```
     = MIN-OF + (MAX-REPS * MAX-NUM)
     Where
     MIN-OF = minimum value of Non-Repeaters field and number of variable
bindings
     MAX-REPS = Max-Repetitions field in request
     MAX-NUM = minimum of number of variable bindings and zero
```

SNMP SET

The SNMP SET command initiates a network management request to remote management agent to change the value of an SNMP Variable. The SET command, when used on a table row that contains multiple variables, will have multiple variables, one for each object, all with the same instance identifier.

In SNMP, at the protocol level, a management station issues an SNMP set operation containing an arbitrary set of variable bindings. In the case where an agent detects that one or more of those variable bindings refer to an object instance not currently available in that agent, it may, according to the rules of the SNMP, behave according to any of the following paradigms:

(1) It may reject the SNMP set operation as referring to non-existent object instances by returning a response with the error-status field set to "noSuchName" and the error-index field set to refer to the first vacuous reference.

(2) It may accept the SNMP set operation as requesting the creation of new object instances corresponding to each of the object instances named in the variable bindings. The value of each (potentially) newly created object instance is specified by the "value" component of the relevant variable binding. In this case, if the request specifies a value for a newly (or previously) created object that it deems inappropriate by reason of value or syntax, then it rejects the SNMP set operation by responding with the error-status field set to badValue and the error-index field set to refer to the first offending variable binding.

(3) It may accept the SNMP set operation and create new object instances as described in (2) above and, in addition, at its discretion, create supplemental object instances to complete a row in a conceptual table of which the new object instances specified in the request may be a part.

From Manager - to Agent

PDU Type 3	Request I.D.	Error Status	Error Index	Object 1 - Value 1	Object n - Value n

From Agent - to Manager

PDU Type 2	Request I.D.	Error Status	Error Index	Object 1 - Value 1	Object n - Value n

Figure 9.4 SNMP SET Request / Response.

The SET command is one of the most difficult to implement within the agent. It is also the most frustrating from the user perspective. It can (and will) return a number of errors to the NMS. Although the errors are similar to the other SNMP commands, they differ enough that they are presented below.

- **Variable Binding error**—this error arises when the variable binding's field is not available for Set operations. The error returned is "noSuchName" with an error index that indicates the variable.

- **Variable Field error**—this error is an indication that the variable binding field does not conform to the TLV requirements. The error returned is "badValue" with the error index set.

- **Size error**—this error indicates that the response PDU would exceed some limitation known to the agent. The error returned is "tooBig" with the error index set to 0 (zero).

- **General Set error**—this error is returned when a variable cannot be altered for whatever reason. The returned error is "genErr" with the appropriate index.

SNMP INFORMREQUEST

InformRequest is used for manager-to-manager communications. This capability could readily be utilized for distributive management as well as providing redundant management. This functionality was introduced for V2 but several vendors are retrofitting V1 with similar functionality.

RESPONSES

One factor not clearly understood is that there is an SNMP Response to every SNMP command. Some believe that commands, such as the SET, do not have a response. It is also thought, by some, that the set should return some indication that the set took place. Neither is correct. A management application should routinely follow a SET with a GET to assure that the value in question was set.

V2 Responses

SNMPv2 agent will not generate a Response-PDU with an error-status field having a value of "noSuchName," "badValue," or "readOnly." These error status were dropped in V2. All of these subtle differences must be addressed by implementors attempting the development of a bilingual agent.

FOR FURTHER STUDY

The following documents contain useful information that is beyond the scope of this chapter.

RFC 1052, NRI. Cerf, V. April 1988. (IAB Recommendations for the Development of Internet Network Management Standards.)

REFERENCES

Case, J., M. Fedor, M. Schoffstall, and J. Davin. *RFC 1157*. (Simple Network Management Protocol.)

10

V1—V2 Coexistence

INTRODUCTION

For the most part I intermingle material from V1 and V2, and up to this point, I have stayed away from many references to SNMPv2 specifics. That was due in part to the fact that there is a general uneasiness with V2. Few vendors and users have shown interest in V2. This is due primarily to the security features that were part of V2. I have always believed that when a piece of software becomes more trouble than it is worth, it will not find the market share it had hoped for. There will be those who will say I am wrong and that the complexity is required, but I will let the sales and implementation numbers speak for me.

The single biggest issue for V2 is the encryption (DES). Not only is it very slow—having been created for hardware implementations—it is also banned from export to many countries. This makes for a sales and marketing nightmare. There are, however, a number of people working on simplified security with several proposals already out. Surely one will provide a workable solution. With that said, I would still be negligent if I did not spend some time talking about V1 to V2 conversion.

There are at least two approaches to dealing with V2, without moving away from V1 completely. These are favorable to the complete conversion because of the need to stay compatible with everybody.

The two approaches that seem to be receiving favor are Bilingual Managers and using Proxy Agents. To fully explore the subject the RFC 1452 that covers the coexistence of V1 and V2, each is presented briefly on the following page.

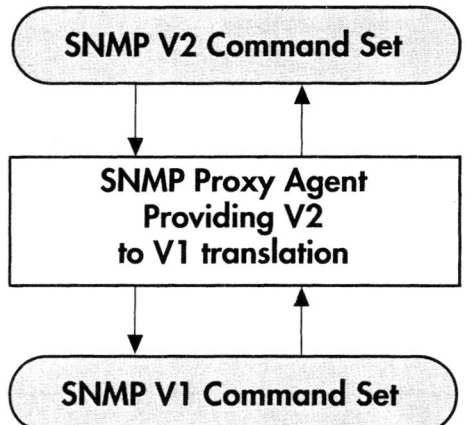

Figure 10.1 Command Mapping

The major enhancements/changes of SNMPv2 are:

- New Macros
- New Data Types
- Textual Conventions
- Manager-to-Manager
- Bulk Transfer
- More Error Codes
- Enhanced Security

Each of these elements is discussed in the text. Most are familiar with the enhanced security and the requirements it places on the development. Many implementations have developed only limited security. Many of the V2 enhancements add complexity. For example, an SNMPv2 entity must be capable of acting as either an agent or manager. This characteristic provides the Manager-to-Manager capability. Other enhancements include the improvements to the SNMP PDUs and additional error codes. The additional error codes allow the NMS to more readily determine why an operation may have failed.

PROXY AGENTS

Proxy agents are described in the RFC 1452 as the approach to the coexistence of V1 and V2. Coexistence is the term used in the RFC, and I love it. It brings to mind two parties that cannot tolerate each other, but somehow manage to coexist. That is, in fact, the case with V1 and V2: they do not communicate with each other without an intermediary (a proxy).

The required characteristics of a proxy agent are covered in the RFC and will not be detailed here. I will, however, touch on some of the high points.

To perform as a proxy agent, the SNMP code must be configured as an agent. Recall the SNMPv2 requires that the code be able to perform as either the agent or manager. In this case, it is performing as an agent that will convert requests from one version to the other. In order to do this correctly, a number of criteria must be met.

- When translating from SNMPv2 to SNMPv2 the agent must:

    (1) If a GetRequest-PDU, GetNextRequest-PDU, or SetRequest-PDU is received, then it is passed unaltered.

    (2) If a GetBulkRequest-PDU is received, the proxy agent sets the non-repeater and max-repetitions fields to zero, and sets the tag of the PDU to GetNextRequest-PDU.

- When translating from SNMPv1 acting as an agent to SNMPv2 acting as a manager, the agent must:

    (1) If a GetResponse-PDU is received, then it is passed unaltered.

    (2) If a Trap-PDU is received, then it is mapped into a SNMPv2-Trap-PDU. This mapping is done via specific rules that are outlined in the RFC. Make sure you have some spare time when you read this part of the RFC; you'll need it.

A number of other considerations are also necessary when constructing a proxy agent. It is a complex effort and should not be taken lightly. The complete details are far outside the scope of this work.

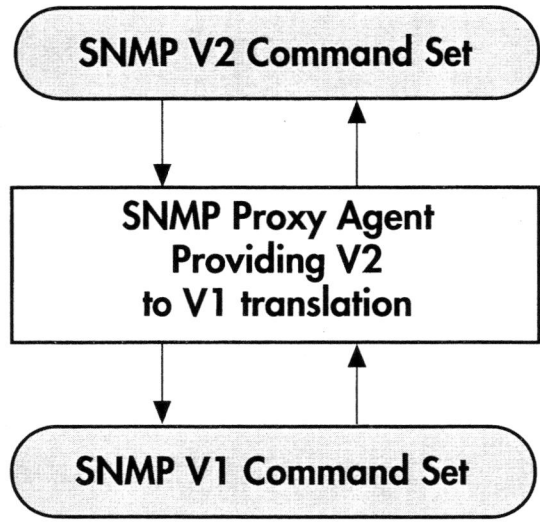

Figure 10.2 Proxy Agent.

Additional Uses for Proxy Agents

Another capability of proxy agents is that they can be developed to talk to non-SNMP management agents. Just as they are used to convert V1 to V2 or vise versa, they can be developed to translate to any management protocol.

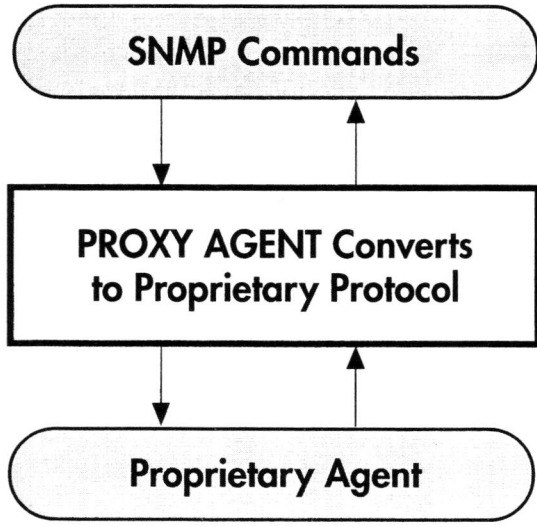

Figure 10.3 Additional Use of Proxy Agent.

Another capability of a proxy is to be able to shield an SNMP agent from access control policies. For example, the proxy could shield the NMS from the complexity of MIB views. Interestingly enough, this has not been implemented to any great extent. The proxy could also shield the agent from redundant requests.

Proxy Agents—Problems

One of the issues that has arisen from the introduction of proxy agents is open access. Through the use of a proxy agent, a vendor can hide the true protocol being used. This allows flexibility, but it also creates a situation in which vendors are more prone to develop a proxy agent than to completely embrace the SNMP environment. At some point this could create a troubling situation, since the protocol will have a number of problems, none of which will have a clear source for solution. One party will point the finger at the next, and the end user will be left with no solutions.

BILINGUAL MANAGERS

Another approach to coexistence of the two versions is the use of a bilingual manager. When a bilingual manager is used, it communicates with an SNMPv1 agent using a V1 protocol. When communicating with an SNMPv2 agent, it will switch to a V2 protocol. When functioning as a V2 manager, the InformRequest can be used. In the administration process of the manager, it is instructed what protocol to use with a given agent. This approach is very flexible, given that it can manage any agent used by any vendor. In this case, the manager accepts the burden of using the correct protocol.

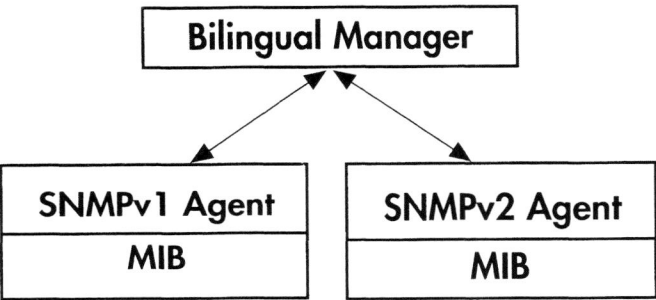

Figure 10.4 Bilingual Manager.

The bilingual manager does not inherently know what command set it should use to communicate with a given agent. They make the determination which version to use for a given agent based upon information contained in the MIB. For example, when communicating with a V2 agent, the InformRequest can be used. When communicating in a V1, mode the InformRequest would not be available.

CONVERSION

If a complete conversion to V2 is required, a good deal of work will be required for the MIB. Much of the early text of this book is related to the SMI/MIB creation. This is due to the fact that it tends to be one of those areas that is often overlooked until someone realizes the magnitude of the effort required. That same level of effort is required for conversion to V2. Below I touch on some of the issues of the conversion.

MIB Conversion

As with everything else relating to SNMP, MIB Conversion is presented in an RFC somewhere, and the RFC is the best source for the complete detail. What is presented here are the key points.

In general, conversion of a MIB module does not require the deprecation of the objects contained therein. Only if the semantics of an object truly change should deprecation be performed.

- The IMPORTS statement must reference SNMPv2-SMI. Many of the V1 implementations referenced RFC1155-SMI and RFC-1212. Just adding SNMPv2-SMI IMPORTs while leaving the other two does not work.

- The MODULE-IDENTITY macro must be invoked immediately after any IMPORTs or exports' statement.

- Hyphen characters must be removed.

- Various SYNTAX clauses must be changed.

- For all objects, the ACCESS clause must be replaced by a MAX-ACCESS clause.

- For any columnar object which is used solely for instance identification in a conceptual row, the object must have the value of its MAX-ACCESS clause set to "not- accessible."

- For all objects, if the value of the STATUS clause is "mandatory," the value must be replaced with "current."

- For all objects, if the value of the STATUS clause is "optional," the value must be replaced with "obsolete."

- For any object not containing a DESCRIPTION clause, the object must have a DESCRIPTION clause defined.

- For any object corresponding to a conceptual row that does not have an INDEX clause, the object must have either an INDEX clause or an AUG-MENTS clause defined.

This is not intended to be complete; it does however, give some idea of the requirements and will get you started. Along with the changes listed, there are a number of changes that are recommended. It has been my experience that when the protocol authors make a recommendation, it should be given due consideration. As with the initial MIB creation, the conversion will require time and effort. Every object in the MIB will need to be reviewed. MIBs containing thousands of objects can require many hours.

FOR FURTHER STUDY

The following documents contain useful information that is beyond the scope of this chapter.

Recommendation X.208. Specification of Abstract Syntax Notation One. (See also ISO 8824.)

REFERENCES

Case, J., K. McCloghrie, M. Rose, and S. Waldbusser. *RFC 1444.* "Conformance Statements for version 2 of the Simple Network Management Protocol (SNMPv2)."

Chen, Tai. *Data Communications*, "Proxy Agents Block SNMP's Open Promise." November 1993.

Fisher, Sharon. *Communications Week*, "Secure SNMP, Anyone." April 4, 1994.

11

V2 Modifications

INTRODUCTION

One of the major changes of V2 is the addition of new data types. V2 has added support for types that were not supported in V1. The ASN.1 types from RFC 1155 that have not changed are INTEGER, OCTET STRING and OBJECT IDENTIFIER. The defined data types from RFC 1155 that have not changed include IpAddress, TimeTicks and Opaque. The data types that are new with SNMPv2 include BIT STRING, Integer32, Counter32, Gauge32, NsapAddress, Counter64 and UIntger32.

Error Codes

Another major change was the addition of more expanative error codes. The changes in the error codes are reflected in Table 11.1.

V2 Error	GET	GETNEXT	GETBULK	SET	INFORM
noErro	✗	✗	✗	✗	✗
tooBig	✗	✗		✗	✗
getErr	✗	✗	✗	✗	
noAcces				✗	
wrongType				✗	
wrongLength				✗	
wrongEncoding				✗	
wrongValue				✗	
noCreation				✗	
inconsistentValue				✗	
resourceUnavailable				✗	
commitFailed				✗	
undoFailed				✗	
authorizationError	✗	✗	✗	✗	✗
notWriteable				✗	
inconsistentName				✗	

Table 11.1 Error Codes

There are three error codes that are never generated in V2, they are:

- noSuchName
- badValue
- readOnly

These error codes were dropped in part for security reasons.

M2M (MANAGER TO MANAGER)

One of the more significant enhancements provided by SNMP v2 is the ability for entities to be configured as either managers or agents. It also implies that two managers can communicate. This manager to manager (M2M) communications can be significant for implementations that want one central manager to communicate to distributed subnets. Such an architecture could be developed utilizing a central manager that talked to distributed managers, each on a subnet. The accompanying software has the MIT agent which can be configured as a manager or agent or both, dependent on the compile flags.

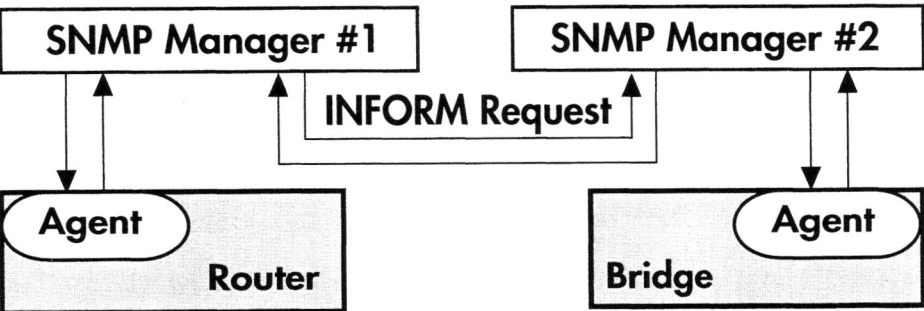

Figure 11.1 Manager to Manager Communication.

The M2M capability is supported by the M2M MIB. The M2M MIB defines procedures for one manager to talk to another manager. To support these procedures, three new concepts were used. They are:

- alarms
- events
- notifications

The alarm is used to trigger an event. The event may cause notifications to be reported to any number of management stations. The information PDU is used for this purpose.

The M2M MIB is divided into groups as we saw with the SNMP–V2 MIB. The groups represent each of the procedures listed above. The groups are:

- **ALARM GROUP**—this group contains information related to configuration threshold alarms for entities acting in a dual, manager/agent, role.

- **EVENT GROUP**—this group provides an event table that associates an event type with a notification.

- **NOTIFICATION GROUP**—provides information related to the notifications.

M2M introduces the ability to provide distributed management. Distributed network managemant is needed and will enhance network management. Most vendors including IBM, HP and AT&T are working on this type of functionality.

V2 SECURITY

The issue of security for V2 is truely a sore spot for many. To implement the complete security requirements for V2 would require a good deal of time and effort. It has been said that an interim step may be forthcoming because of the complexity of V2 security. The reader should consult the latest information on the Internet before going too far with V2 security. I ended up getting one of those little, frustration-relieving, punching dolls when I first started dealing with V2 security.

The Authentication Protocol provides a mechanism by which SNMPv2 management communications transmitted by the party may be reliably identified as having originated from that party. The authentication protocol reliably determines that the message received is the message that was sent.

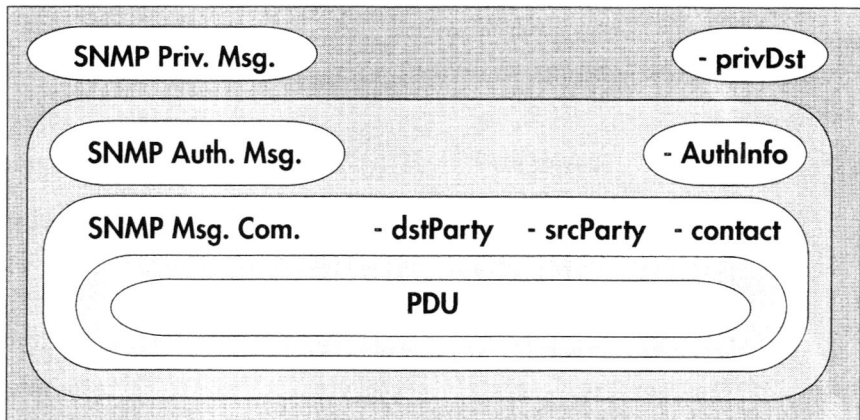

Figure 11.2   V2 Security Envelope.

The Symmetric Privacy Protocol protects messages from disclosure by encrypting their contents according to a secret cryptographic key known only to the originator and recipient. The additional functionality afforded by this protocol is assumed to justify its additional computational cost.

The Digest Authentication Protocol depends on the existence of loosely synchronized clocks between the originator and recipient of a message. The protocol specification makes no assumptions about the strategy by which such clocks are synchronized.

The three paragraphs above are excerpts from the RFC 1446. They provide a bit of the flavor of V2 security. They also start to give the reader an idea of the pain involved with V2 security. That pain grows when the implementor realizes that there are export rules that come into play with the use of the encryption algorithm (DES) outlined in V2. To add to the problem, the CPU cycles required to utilize DES are extreme for an embedded real time system. The CPU requirements became clear to me in a recent implementation. When the system was at 75 percent of capacity and it received an SNMPv2 PDU, it would immediately go 100 percent busy and begin to drop the network traffic. This was not exactly what the client wanted to see. It didn't do much for my day, either.

DES is Data Encryption Standard and the specifications for it are published by at least two sources:

- National Institute of Standards and Technology

- American National Standards Institute

A working version of DES code is included on the accompanying source diskettes.

When Privacy is used, the entire PDU, except for the 'priv Dst' field is ASN.1 encoded. The Privacy Protocol will utilize three variables, 'party Priv Protocol,' 'party Priv Private' and 'party Priv Public.' These variables are kept in the Party Database. The database contains information about each 'Party' in the form of five authentication variables. The variables, 'party Auth Protocol,' 'party Auth Lifetime.' The authentication mechanism, MD5, utilizes these variables. MD5 provides for the verification of the integrity of the message.

The Access Control has four components, 'Destination Party,' 'Source Party,' 'Resources' and 'Privileges.' The access control is provided through the use of these elements and there may be multiple access control policies. through the four tables in the Party MIB access privileges can be determined. The four MIB control tables are, 'party table,' 'context table,' 'access control table' and the 'MIB view tables.'

privDst	authinfo	dstParty	srcParty	context	SNMP Data

Basic Format

privDst	0 - length Octet String	dstParty	srcParty	context	SNMP Data

Unsecured Message

privDst	digest	dstTimestamp	srcTimestamp	dstParty	srcParty	context	SNMP Data

Authenticated - Non Private Message

privDst	0 - length Octet String	dstParty	srcParty	context	SNMP Data

Private - Non Authenticated Message

privDst	digest	dstTimestamp	srcTimestamp	dstParty	srcParty	context	SNMP Data

Authenticated and Private Message

Figure 11.3 SNMPv2 Message Security Formats

FOR FURTHER STUDY

The following documents contain useful information that is beyond the scope of this chapter.

Document	Description
ISO 3307, Information interchange	Representations of time of the day.
ISO 4031, Information interchange	Representation of local time differentials.
ISO 6523, Data interchange	Structure for identification of organizations.

Data Encryption Standard, National Institute of Standards and Technology. Federal Information Processing Standard (FIPS) Publication 46-1.

ANSI X3.92-1981, (December, 1980)	Data Encryption Algorithm, American National Standards Institute
(FIPS) Publication 81, December, 1980)	DES Modes of Operation, National Institute of Standards and Technology. Federal Information Processing Standard
ANSI X3.106-1983 (May 1983)	Data Encryption Algorithm Modes of Operation, American

12

Other Transport Protocols

INTRODUCTION

SNMP was originally developed to utilize UDP, although some consideration was given to the possibility that it might be used with other transport protocols. Remember that SNMP was only intended to be an interim solution so other transports did not appear to be a main concern. As SNMP has taken more and more of a foothold, the need for the comparability with other transport protocols has grown and grown. A number of RFCs being generated that outlines the use of SNMP with other transports. Currently there are RFCs for SNMP over OSI, SNMP over AppleTalk, SNMP over IPX, with others proposed. One of the original SNMP RFCs, RFC 1089 (SNMP over Ethernet) provides insight to the requirements of SNMP.

Many of the SNMP agents do not have the hooks for utilizing transports other than UDP, and they are not very amenable to any attempt to change that. Others have most of the interface isolated and can be easily adapted to other transports. No matter what transport protocol is utilized the key factor is the support of the five properties listed in Chapter 4. Again they are:

- End-to-End Checksum
- Multiplexing/Demultiplexing
- Routing
- Media Independence
- Fragmentation and Reassembly

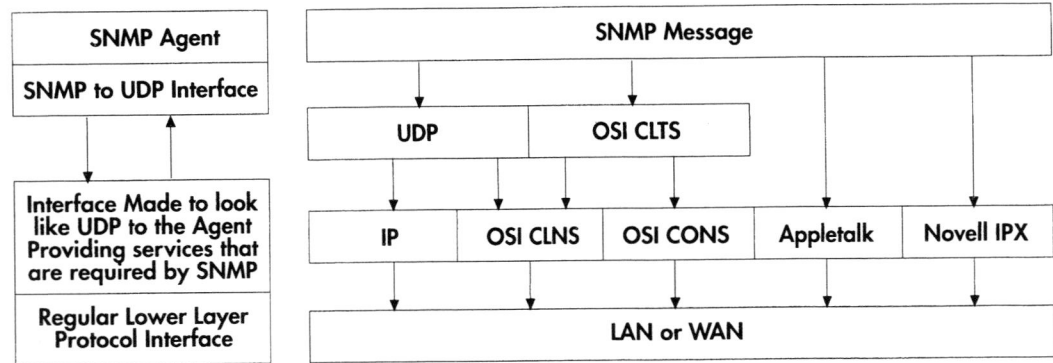

Figure 12.1 MultiProtocol Layering.

One example of an agent that can be adapted to other protocols is the MIT version included on the accompanying diskette. The interface (below) is easily modified to make a call to other transports without changing the agent or the transport.

```
SmpStatusType udpSend (udp, bp, n)

SmpSocketType          udp;
CBytePtrType           bp;
CIntfType              n;

{
      UdpPtrType              tp;
      int                     result;

      if (udp == (SmpSocketType) 0) {
            return (errBad);
      }

      tp = (UdpPtrType) udp;
      do {
            result = sendto (tp->udpSocket, (char *) bp,
                  (int) n, (int) 0,
                  & (tp->udpSockAddr), sizeof (struct sockaddr_in));
            n -= result;
            bp += result;

      } while ((result > 0) && (n > 0));

      if (result < 0) {
            perror ("udpSend");
            return (errBad);
      }
```

```
      else {
            return (errOk);
      }
}
```

A quick and dirty implementation would be to replace the area in bold type with some other protocol or possibly a subroutine that handled the new protocol gracefully. True, this is a fairly "dirty" approach that should only be utilized for prototyping, but it demonstrates the area where the developer could attack.

Using Multiple Protocols

Often the SNMP agent is required to be able to use multiple protocols. This happens when there is a need to have an out-of-band channel for communications. There will generally be an in-band and out-of-band, both, with SNMP communications required. This is a challenge for all but the best commercial SNMP agents. It can become very complex if the agent is on an embedded system and must be able to route the SNMP response back on any available route. That is to say, the original in path may have hung, and the routing needs to take a different route and protocol back to the initiator.

Many problems can arise when utilizing multiple protocols. Multiple protocol stacks within the same environment tend to cause memory issue, buffer conflicts, duplicate infrastructures and transport bound applications. The co-residence of multiple protocols also tends to eat CPU cycles and cause still other problems. From a development perspective multiple protocols require additional support as well as the additional burden of version and release control. Even with all of these issues, many vendors find it to be worthwhile to enhance SNMP with added transport protocols. In some cases it can and should be done, but the cost must be understood.

Other transports that have gained a great deal of interest for use with SNMP are SLIP and PPP. This allows vendors to dial up their clients around the world to assist with management of unruly systems. These protocols will be covered in some detail later in this chapter.

X.25

A native X.25 implementation of SNMP would be extremely difficult, requiring a great deal of code and work. It would require the understanding and implementation of X.121, the X.25 addressing scheme. All of this is outside the scope of this work, however, there is an approach to utilizing X.25, to utilize "tunneling."

Tunneling

Tunneling is the use of X.25 simply as a delivery vehicle. It is done by making an X.25 connection and then sending the UDP/IP packets across as though they were a form of data. The down side of this approach is that some type of equipment must be used to make the X.25 connect with and host the UDP/IP data. This approach is in popular demand for SNMP because of the wide coverage and availability of X.25.

LLC and LLC2

The developer should not need to know what the second layer protocol is. That should be the case when LLC is utilized, but on occasion LLC will create some difficulty. SNMP should not tie itself to any Layer Two protocol, and LLC is no exception. The primary reason for their inclusion here is to consider LLC2 which does "spoofing" of the various end point equipment.

LLC and LLC2 are protocol layers that are clearly defined by the IEEE 802 project. LLC defines a connectionless protocol, while LLC2 defines the same protocol with enhancements to support the connection oriented model. LLC lives and breathes under many versions of token-ring but is seldom utilized with Ethernet or 802.3. (Ethernet is the DIX base of 802.3). LLC2 is not often implemented because of the complexity involved with "spoofing" on when an unreliable media is used.

Developers should consult the appropriate RFC related to using SNMP with the transport protocol they intend to use. It is also appropriate to refer to any documents relating to that specific transport. The developer should also consider the use of encapsulation. That is the process of placing the entire SNMP PDU in the data segment of a transport, and letting the transport carry the SNMP data without further knowledge of the fact that it is carrying a complete PDU. This method is often used for ISO implementations and can just as easily be utilized with SNMP. It provides a fast method for development, and in cases where the transport source is not available, it is the only way to achieve an implementation.

SLIP and PPP

SLIP (Serial Line /IP) and PPP (Point to Point Protocol) are very popular protocols that are utilized a great deal in the embedded systems world. PPP tends to be used with local consoles while SLIP primarily serves as a means by which a dial up connection can be made. The dial up connection can serve as a means for a vendor to trouble shoot networking equipment without being on site or as an out-of-band connection.

To implement SLIP or PPP in an SNMP agent the methodology is similar. Either protocol must be mapped into the UDP mentality of SNMP. Depending on how far the developer wants to go for a clean implementation the size of the task will vary. In those cases where the implementor needs a fast turn, the same approach that was outlined in the beginning of this chapter could be used. In those cases where the implementation needs to be pristine the developer may need to add some type of logic to support a type of addressing algorithm.

VARIOUS TRANSPORT PROTOCOL

Some of the transport protocols we have mentioned were given no more than a single paragraph. That really was all that was required since the data is merely the cargo for most transport layers. The transport protocol itself has little or no knowledge of the cargo.

SNMP provides the ASN.1 encoding before the data is passed to the transport. Various layers of the transport may do further encoding of headers into ASN.1 yet that has no affect on SNMP.

When utilizing other transport layers, the main concern should be adapting the API (Application Programming Interface) from SNMP to the transport interface. If the transport happens to utilize ASN.1 encoding, the developer will need to assure that BEDLs (Basic Encoding and Decoding Library) is compatible across the transport interface.

The developer will also need to recognize the type of transport interface that is native to the target system. For example, an agent being developed for System V UNIX would probably utilize the TLI (Transport Layer Interface) rather then Berkeley Sockets. In other cases the use of the file abstraction may be most appropriate. The exact interface is dependent on the target system.

FOR FURTHER STUDY

The following documents contain useful information that is beyond the scope of this chapter.

Document	Description
Data Communications Computer Networks and Open Systems	Third Addition by F. Halsall
"Connectionless Network Protocol (ISO 8473)	by Satz, G

"SNMP over Ethernet," RFC 1089 February 1989	by Schoffstall, M., Davin, C.,Fedor, M., and J. Case
RFC 793 September 1981	by Postel, J., "Transmission Control Protocol"
RFC 768	by Postel, J., [5] "User Datagram Protocol"
RFC 1449	"Transport Mappings for version 2 of the Simple Network Management Protocol (SNMPv2)" Case, J., McCloghrie, K., Rose, M., and Waldbusser, S.,
Principles of Communication and Networking Protocols ©Computer Society Press 1984	by Simon Lam
SNA Perspective August 1992 ©CSI	IBM

REFERENCES

Stallings, W. *Handbook of Computer Communications* (Three Volumes). Macmillan Publishing, 1987.

13

An Agent

Other chapters have focused on developing the periphery of an agent. The point being that the knowledge simply is not there yet. The thinking seems to be to focus on the detail of the SNMP protocol rather than delivering functionality that utilized with the SNMP protocol. Every single agent could easily do a warm boot of a piece of equipment. Looking at the code, below:

```
#define MAGIC            0                /* for cold restart */
/* #define MAGIC          0x1234          /* for warm restart */

#define BOOT_SEG   0xffffL
#define BOOT_OFF   0x0000L
#define BOOT_ADR   ((BOOT_SEG << 16) | BOOT_OFF)

#define DOS_SEG            0x0040L
#define RESET_FLAG  0x0072L
#define RESET_ADR   ((DOS_SEG << 16) | RESET_FLAG)

static MixStatusType   sysBootSet (cookie, name, namelen, asn)

MixCookieType       cookie;
MixNamePtrType      name;
MixLengthType       namelen;
AsnIdType           asn;

{
     cookie = cookie;
     name = name;
     namelen = namelen;
     asn = asn;
     void ((far *fp)()) = (void (far *)()) BOOT_ADR;
```

```
/*
          Could add a great deal to make the
          system happy before the boot is done.
*/

*(int far *)RESET_ADR = MAGIC;
(*fp)();
return 0;        /* never gets here, but keeps compiler happy */
}
```

It can be seen that a developer could readily do a warm boot. Such functionality would be exercised by doing an SNMP Set of the variable by the NMS. The set would transcend the network and trigger the code to do the warm boot.

Let's now look at the flow of the set through the agent. We will utilize the flow of the MIT agent code included on the diskette. That code is an excellent example since it is the base code utilized by HP, AT&T and IBM in their agent products.

Note: All three of these vendors have multiple agents to analyze an agent problem without being sure that the agent uses this code base.

We will begin analyzing the agent with the receipt of the PDU. Ethernet, IP, UDP are assumed.

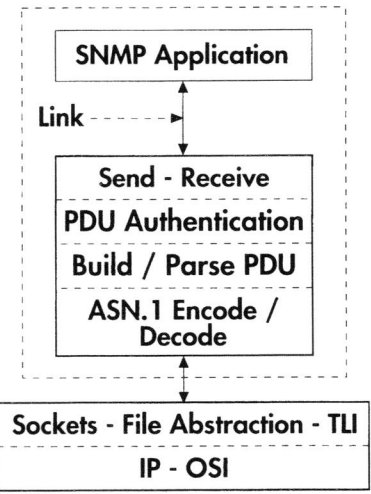

Figure 13.1 Architecture.

The SNMP agent at start up will bind to the appropriate port filling a socket structure with the appropriate information. This socket abstraction is often an area for problems. Many have utilized differing socket structures and often the fields simply do not match. In other cases there will be discrepancies in network address field of this structure. The return address is taken from the incoming packet. This allows the SNMP response to get back to the correct manager. This can be utilized for dealing with multiple managers.

After the agent stores off this information it will begin the process of decoding the SNMP PDU. In the debug code presented in the appendix it can be seen that the agent will go through many cycles to decode the PDU. The agent will evaluate the data as the decoding takes place. The agent walks the OID tree as the decoding happens. Should the agent find that the OID does not exist in the MIB the agent will stop decoding and return the appropriate message. If the decoding completes the agent will know exactly what MIB element is the target of the PDU.

With the agent now having a handle on the MIB element it will exercise logic to determine what can be done with this element. The element may be READ ONLY and the PDU was a set.

The agent would reject the set returning the appropriate message to the NMS. The information relating to the MIB element is contained in the MIB structure. Every element of the MIB will consist of a structure with the basic information relating to that element.

```
typedef struct MibStrTag{
                        CUnsfType    mibStrMaxLen;
                        CUnsfType    mibStrLen;
                        CBytePtr     mibStrData;
                        } MibStrType;
typedef MibStrType *MibStrPtrType;


MibStatusType   mibIntlRW();
MibStatusType   mib;ntlRO();
```

Figure 13.2 Internal MIB Structure.

Every agent will utilize some different structure to maintain MIB information. Some agents provide the ability to extend the MIB. The MIT agent does not since it is intended to be an embedded agent and not expanded when in use.

At this point the agent knows what can be done with the target MIB element. If the SNMP PDU is a GET REQUEST the MIB structure will be accessed via a pointer. That pointer in the MIT MIB can be a pointer to a function. That function would execute and return the appropriate value. Since the MIT agent uses an assignment of the pointer value, the return of the function is assigned as well. That return value, after being assigned, is the actual MIB variable. Generally this variable is named by the MIB element name. In some cases the MIB pointer will be a pointer to a value that is to be updated by other parts of the system. Generally such updates will be outside the scope of the agent. Bad values in these elements are often attributed to the agent. Many will observe values that are not correct and make a statement about the quality of the agent when it is actually the surrounding system at fault.

Now that the agent has the value for the MIB element it begins the process of encoding the value. The first step associated with encoding is to add a type field. Then to begin the encoding. Upon completion of the encoding the value is placed in a buffer. A pointer to the buffer is then given to the appropriate transport protocol. The transport protocol was stored during the receipt of the SNMP PDU. Since the MIT code functions in this manner, there may be multiple transport protocols utilized at the same time. This is ideal for providing out-of-band backup or dial up management.

The MIT agent is structured to run to completion. That is, the PDUs are serialized. Most agents function in this manner to assure that conflicting requests are not processed out of the sequence received.

Some functionality that is not available in the MIT agent includes the ability to unwind variables or do a test of a variable. Both of these relate to SNMPv1's requirement that all variables of a SET multiple binding be set or none are set.

The main objection to the MIT code is its complexity. It is highly portable taking less than a week to port to PSOS and Vertex. It ports to DOS as a TSR and with a little care it can be built in to an executable that is only 32K. This small size and great portability make it an excellent starting point for an agent implementation. Documentation is a bit slim but can be found in a commercial form.

Although there is no compiler with the MIT agent there are several GDMO compilers available.

The code is structured into directories as seen below:

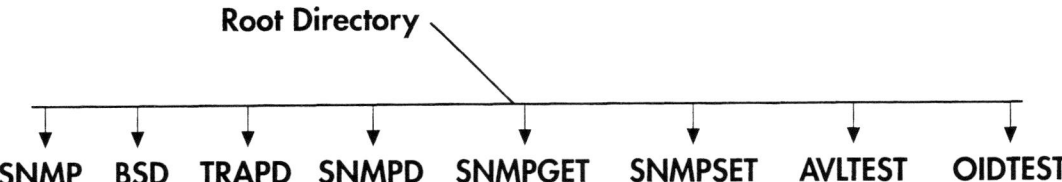

Figure 13.3 Directory Structure.

Each directory is specific to the functionality. The SNMP directory builds all of the encoding and decoding logic into a library. The BSD directory provides all the logic to link with Berkeley Sockets. SNMPD will link with SNMP and BSD to provide an agent to run on a Berkeley type system. TRAPD will link with SNMP and BSD to provide a TRAP demon. SNMPGET and SNMPSET will link with SNMP GET and SET functions. There are also test directories (not listed) that can be used to test the builds and the functionality.

The MIT agent can readily be coupled to the BTREE software included on the diskette. The BTREE software can be coupled to a GDMO compiler output to provide an agent and compiler package equal to the $30,000.00 commercial packages. Utilizing this code, an intelligent MIB based on information in this book, a completed agent can be done for under $5000.00. It will function better than the commercial versions and it will be your own.

FOR FURTHER STUDY

The following documents contain useful information that is beyond the scope of this chapter.

Document	Description
MIT Documentation	On Diskette

REFERENCES

Case, J., M. Fedor, M. Schoffstall, and J. Davin. *RFC 1157* "Simple Network Management Protocol."

APPENDIX A

NSFNET—Information

The day-to-day operations of NSFNET are done by MERIT at Ann Arbor, Michigan. A new Network Operations Center (NOC) in the University of Michigan's Computing Center Building is the focus of the daily operations. Under the supervision of engineers, technicians and operators the hardware and software of the NSFNET is monitored and maintained. The NOC provides round the clock operations and control.

Merit produces and delivers on-line information about the network and assists technical personnel at the middle level sites. Information files are available for anonymous FTP from Merit/NSFNET Information Services machine. An electronic newsletter, The Link Letter, is published monthly with technical articles and features about the NSFNET.

You can reach the Merit/NSFNET Information services at:

Phone:	(800) 66-MERIT
Electronic Mail:	NSFNET-Info@merit.edu
U.S. Mail:	Merit/NSFNET Information Services
	1075 Beal Avenue
	Ann Arbor, Michigan 48109-2112

APPENDIX B

SNMP Implementations of Note

This appendix relates to the various SNMP implementations. It is not intended to cover every one, just some of the more successful ones. "Successful" here means market share and does not relate to quality; that evaluation will have to come from the long-term users of these implementations.

MACSNMP

The implementation of SNMP for the Macintosh computer is called MacSNMP and consists of a number of components. It is capable of dealing with its own MIB and third-party MIBs. The manager operates over both AppleTalk and straight TCP/IP.

NOTE: AppleTalk is an off shoot of TCP/IP.

MacSNMP is also supported by Apple Internet Router.

CABLETRON SYSTEMS INC.

Cabletron Spectrum, Remote LANview Windows, and MIB Navigator are all available from Cabletron, and they allow managers to work with the MIB and various configuration information. Primarily targeted at the Cabletron platforms, the tools are available for use with third-party equipment.

DEC POLYCENTER

Digital Equipment has been known for distributed interconnect. In years past the standing line was "if you want to connect two different systems, do it through a DEC system." The DEC SNMP implementation is no different in that it operates under the EMA (Enterprise Management Architecture). PolyCenter runs on virtually all of the DEC platforms. The manager supports a number of the OSI management components. The EMA operates as an environment that allows a number of "presentation" modules to operate.

HEWLETT-PACKARD CO.

Hewlett-Packard has taken the lead in UNIX, quietly selling more UNIX products than any other vendor. HP is showing the same competitiveness in the SNMP management arena. Every development lab that I go to seems to have at least one HP OpenView platform. HP has taken several different approaches to SNMP management. It offers the base product as well as a distributed OpenView product. The API (Application Programmers Interface) is very complete and the overall system is very good. This has led to HP's product being relabeled and sold by a number of other vendors. OpenView is based upon an object-oriented approach with the various objects registering through an Object Registration Service. This service provides such things as mapping the names to network addresses. HP also provides a MIB browser that is a very useful tool.

IBM

IBM System Monitor/6000 runs on AIX, providing a user interface to various agents and network components. This product has some capabilities that many of the other implementations simply do not support. That is due to the fact that it utilizes three types of interfaces. One interface provides a centralized mentality. This interface has lent itself to integration into the SNA world. The SNMP Traps can be converted to SNA alerts and vise versa. The system also has strong device discovery capability. It also provides network monitoring for fault and performance measurements. This product will probably remain one of the only manager in the SNA arena for some time because of the difficulty relating to LLC2.

AT&T/NCR ONEVISION

One Vision is a port of HP OpenView, as is the IBM implementation. It offers a few enhancements, but for the most part IBM, AT&T, and HP are all the same. HP is clearly in the lead since it has the development before the IBM and AT&T, but it is quickly ported and the three stay fairly consistent.

NOVELL NETWARE MANAGER

Novell's NetWare Management System provides integrated network management for NetWare LANs. Support for some third-party hubs and routers is also available. The MIBs are loaded as NLMs (Network Loadable Modules) on the server.

SUNCONNECT SUNNET MANAGER

SunNet Manager comes from SunConnect, a division of Sun Microsystems, Inc. It is that separation that has driven the product to be developed to deal with any agent, regardless of the vendor. SunNet has strict adherence to the Internet standards which helps it to achieve this compatibility. SunNet Manager will operate across various protocols. It was developed around an object-oriented philosophy that provides a good deal of functionality. It allows the user to define macros and has such tools as a MIB browser and 3-dimensional graphics for presentation.

CASTLE ROCK SNMPc

SNMPc is a PC-based management application that has gained a lot of popularity because of its price. It is not only inexpensive, but offers a great deal of functionality. It is somewhat simpler to setup than some of the larger network management applications while having all the functionality of a larger network. The maps and services are every bit that of any of the larger applications.

APPENDIX C

SNMPv2 Related RFCs

Introduction to version 2 of the
Internet-standard Network Management Framework

Request for Comments: 1441 April 1993

Authors:

J. Case	SNMP Research, Inc.
K. McCloghrie	Hughes LAN Systems
M. Rose	Dover Beach Consulting, Inc.
S. Waldbusser	Carnegie Mellon University

Structure of Management Information
for version 2 of the Simple Network Management Protocol (SNMPv2)

Request for Comments: 1442 April 1993

Authors:

J. Case	SNMP Research, Inc.
K. McCloghrie	Hughes LAN Systems
M. Rose	Dover Beach Consulting, Inc.
S. Waldbusser	Carnegie Mellon University

Textual Conventions for version 2 of the
Simple Network Management Protocol (SNMPv2)

Request for Comments: 1443 April 1993

Authors:

J. Case	SNMP Research, Inc.
K. McCloghrie	Hughes LAN Systems
M. Rose	Dover Beach Consulting, Inc.
S. Waldbusser	Carnegie Mellon University

Conformance Statements for version 2 of the
Simple Network Management Protocol (SNMPv2)

Request for Comments: 1444 April 1993

Authors:

J. Case	SNMP Research, Inc.
K. McCloghrie	Hughes LAN Systems
M. Rose	Dover Beach Consulting, Inc.
S. Waldbusser	Carnegie Mellon University

Administrative Model for version 2 of the
Simple Network Management Protocol (SNMPv2)

Request for Comments: 1445 April 1993

Authors:

J. Galvin	Trusted Information Systems
K. McCloghrie	Hughes LAN Systems

Security Protocols for version 2 of the
Simple Network Management Protocol (SNMPv2)

Request for Comments: 1446 April 1993

Authors:

J. Galvin   Trusted Information Systems

K. McCloghrie   Hughes LAN Systems

Party MIB for version 2 of the
Simple Network Management Protocol (SNMPv2)

Request for Comments: 1447 April 1993

Authors:

J. Galvin   Trusted Information Systems

K. McCloghrie   Hughes LAN Systems

Protocol Operations for version 2 of the
Simple Network Management Protocol (SNMPv2)

Request for Comments: 1448 April 1993

Authors:

J. Case   SNMP Research, Inc.

K. McCloghrie   Hughes LAN Systems

M. Rose   Dover Beach Consulting, Inc.

S. Waldbusser   Carnegie Mellon University

Transport Mappings for version 2 of the
Simple Network Management Protocol (SNMPv2)

Request for Comments: 1449 April 1993

Authors:

J. Case	SNMP Research, Inc.
K. McCloghrie	Hughes LAN Systems
M. Rose	Dover Beach Consulting, Inc.
S. Waldbusser	Carnegie Mellon University

Management Information Base for version 2 of the
Simple Network Management Protocol (SNMPv2)

Request for Comments: 1450 April 1993

Authors:

J. Case	SNMP Research, Inc.
K. McCloghrie	Hughes LAN Systems
M. Rose	Dover Beach Consulting, Inc.
S. Waldbusser	Carnegie Mellon University

APPENDIX D

DEBUG Output From NMS

Below is the output from the debug of an SNMP SET operation.

```
smpRequest:
asnAppend:
head:
[ C 3 ] SEQUENCE {
}
item:
[ U 2 ] INTEGER {
        00
}
result:
[ C 3 ] SEQUENCE {
        [ U 2 ] INTEGER {
                00
        }
}
asnAppend:
head:
[ C 3 ] SEQUENCE {
        [ U 2 ] INTEGER {
                00
        }
}
item:
[ U 2 ] INTEGER {
        00
}
result:
[ C 3 ] SEQUENCE {
        [ U 2 ] INTEGER {
                00
```

```
                    }
                    [ U 2 ] INTEGER {
                            00
                    }
            }
            asnAppend:
            head:
            [ C 3 ] SEQUENCE {
                    [ U 2 ] INTEGER {
                            00
                    }
                    [ U 2 ] INTEGER {
                            00
                    }
            }
            item:
            [ U 2 ] INTEGER {
                    00
            }
            result:
            [ C 3 ] SEQUENCE {
                    [ U 2 ] INTEGER {
                            00
                    }
                    [ U 2 ] INTEGER {
                            00
                    }
                    [ U 2 ] INTEGER {
                            00
                    }
            }
            asnAppend:
            head:
            [ C 3 ] SEQUENCE {
                    [ U 2 ] INTEGER {
                            00
                    }
                    [ U 2 ] INTEGER {
                            00
                    }
                    [ U 2 ] INTEGER {
                            00
                    }
            }
            item:
            [ U 16 ] SEQUENCE {
            }
            result:
            [ C 3 ] SEQUENCE {
                    [ U 2 ] INTEGER {
                            00
```

```
        }
        [ U 2 ] INTEGER {
                00
        }
        [ U 2 ] INTEGER {
                00
        }
        [ U 16 ] SEQUENCE {
        }
}
result: 00011748
smpSend:
asnAppend:
head:
[ U 16 ] SEQUENCE {
}
item:
[ U 2 ] INTEGER {
        00
}
result:
[ U 16 ] SEQUENCE {
        [ U 2 ] INTEGER {
                00
        }
}
asnAppend:
head:
[ U 16 ] SEQUENCE {
        [ U 2 ] INTEGER {
                00
        }
}
item:
[ U 4 ] OCTETSTRING {
        70 75 62 6C 69 63
}
result:
[ U 16 ] SEQUENCE {
        [ U 2 ] INTEGER {
                00
        }
        [ U 4 ] OCTETSTRING {
                70 75 62 6C 69 63
        }
}
asnAppend:
head:
[ U 16 ] SEQUENCE {
        [ U 2 ] INTEGER {
                00
```

```
        }
        [ U 4 ] OCTETSTRING {
                70 75 62 6C 69 63
        }
}
item:
[ C 3 ] SEQUENCE {
        [ U 2 ] INTEGER {
                00
        }
        [ U 2 ] INTEGER {
                00
        }
        [ U 2 ] INTEGER {
                00
        }
        [ U 16 ] SEQUENCE {
        }
}
result:
[ U 16 ] SEQUENCE {
        [ U 2 ] INTEGER {
                00
        }
        [ U 4 ] OCTETSTRING {
                70 75 62 6C 69 63
        }
        [ C 3 ] SEQUENCE {
                [ U 2 ] INTEGER {
                        00
                }
                [ U 2 ] INTEGER {
                        00
                }
                [ U 2 ] INTEGER {
                        00
                }
                [ U 16 ] SEQUENCE {
                }
        }
}
[ U 16 ] SEQUENCE {
        [ U 2 ] INTEGER {
                00
        }
        [ U 4 ] OCTETSTRING {
                70 75 62 6C 69 63
        }
        [ C 3 ] SEQUENCE {
                [ U 2 ] INTEGER {
                        00
```

```
            }
            [ U  2 ] INTEGER {
                    00
            }
            [ U  2 ] INTEGER {
                    00
            }
            [ U 16 ] SEQUENCE {
            }
      }
}

30 18 02 01 00 04 06 70 75 62 6C 69 63 A3 0B 02 01 00 02 01 00 02 01 00 30 00
udpSend:
30 18 02 01 00 04 06 70 75 62 6C 69 63 A3 0B 02 01 00 02 01 00 02 01 00 30 00
30 18 02 01 00 04 06 70 75 62 6C 69 63 A2 0B 02 01 00 02 01 00 02 01 00 30 00
asnNew dp 106B0
asnType0
asnType0 dp 106B0 np A718
aslChoice 1
asnLen0 asnLenVerify Max -1 Tot 2 Len 24 Min 20 4 4
asnSeq 4
asnPush
asnType0
asnType0 dp 10688 np A738
aslChoice 1
asnLen0 asnLenVerify Max 24 Tot 2 Len 1 Min 1 4 4
asnInteger0: 00
asnInteger1: 00
asnInteger0: 4
asnInteger0: 00010688
asnInteger1: 00
asnInteger0: 2
asnInteger1: 100
asnInteger1: 00
asnInteger1: 4
asnInteger1: 00010688
asnInteger1: 1
asnPop
asnSeq 4
asnPush
asnType0
asnType0 dp 10660 np A758
aslChoice 1
asnLen0 asnLenVerify Max 21 Tot 2 Len 6 Min 0 4 4
asnInteger2: 2
asnInteger2: 2
asnInteger2: 2
asnInteger2: 2
asnInteger2: 2
asnInteger2: 1
```

```
asnPop
asnSeq 4
asnPush
asnType0
asnType0 dp 10638 np A778
aslChoice 1
asnLen0 asnLenVerify Max 13 Tot 2 Len 11 Min 12 4 4
asnSeq 4
asnPush
asnType0
asnType0 dp 10610 np A7D8
aslChoice 1
asnLen0 asnLenVerify Max 11 Tot 2 Len 1 Min 1 4 4
asnInteger0: 00
asnInteger1: 00
asnInteger0: 17
asnInteger0: 00010610
asnInteger1: 00
asnInteger0: 2
asnInteger1: 100
asnInteger1: 00
asnInteger1: 17
asnInteger1: 00010610
asnInteger1: 1
asnPop
asnSeq 4
asnPush
asnType0
asnType0 dp 105E8 np A7F8
aslChoice 1
asnLen0 asnLenVerify Max 8 Tot 2 Len 1 Min 1 4 4
asnInteger0: 00
asnInteger1: 00
asnInteger0: 20
asnInteger0: 000105E8
asnInteger1: 00
asnInteger0: 2
asnInteger1: 100
asnInteger1: 00
asnInteger1: 20
asnInteger1: 000105E8
asnInteger1: 1
asnPop
asnSeq 4
asnPush
asnType0
asnType0 dp 105C0 np A818
aslChoice 1
asnLen0 asnLenVerify Max 5 Tot 2 Len 1 Min 1 4 4
asnInteger0: 00
asnInteger1: 00
```

```
asnInteger0: 23
asnInteger0: 000105C0
asnInteger1: 00
asnInteger0: 2
asnInteger1: 100
asnInteger1: 00
asnInteger1: 23
asnInteger1: 000105C0
asnInteger1: 1
asnPop
asnSeq 4
asnPush
asnType0
asnType0 dp 10598 np A838
aslChoice 1
asnLen0 asnLenVerify Max 2 Tot 2 Len 0 Min 0 4 4
asnSeqOf
asnPop
asnSeq 2
asnPop
asnSeq 2
asnPop
asnDecode bytesLeft 3814
smpInputEvent [ C 2 ] SEQUENCE {
      [ U 2 ] INTEGER {
             00
      }
      [ U 2 ] INTEGER {
             00
      }
      [ U 2 ] INTEGER {
             00
      }
      [ U 16 ] SEQUENCE OF {
      }
}
Request Id: 0
Error: noError
Index: 0
Count: 0

4
result: 0
```

Below is the output from the debug of an SNMP GET of a nonexistent OID.

```
smpRequest:
asnAppend:
head:
[ U 16 ] SEQUENCE {
}
item:
[ U 6 ] OBJECTIDENTIFIER {
        90 49
}
result:
[ U 16 ] SEQUENCE {
        [ U 6 ] OBJECTIDENTIFIER {
                90 49
        }
}
asnAppend:
head:
[ U 16 ] SEQUENCE {
        [ U 6 ] OBJECTIDENTIFIER {
                90 49
        }
}
item:
[ U 4 ] OCTETSTRING {

}
result:
[ U 16 ] SEQUENCE {
        [ U 6 ] OBJECTIDENTIFIER {
                90 49
        }
        [ U 4 ] OCTETSTRING {

        }
}
asnAppend:
head:
[ U 16 ] SEQUENCE {
}
item:
[ U 16 ] SEQUENCE {
        [ U 6 ] OBJECTIDENTIFIER {
                90 49
        }
        [ U 4 ] OCTETSTRING {

        }
}
result:
```

```
[ U 16 ] SEQUENCE {
      [ U 16 ] SEQUENCE {
            [ U 6 ] OBJECTIDENTIFIER {
                        90 49
            }
            [ U 4 ] OCTETSTRING {

            }
      }
}
asnAppend:
head:
[ C 0 ] SEQUENCE {
}
item:
[ U 2 ] INTEGER {
      00
}
result:
[ C 0 ] SEQUENCE {
      [ U 2 ] INTEGER {
            00
      }
}
asnAppend:
head:
[ C 0 ] SEQUENCE {
      [ U 2 ] INTEGER {
            00
      }
}
item:
[ U 2 ] INTEGER {
      00
}
result:
[ C 0 ] SEQUENCE {
      [ U 2 ] INTEGER {
            00
      }
      [ U 2 ] INTEGER {
            00
      }
}
asnAppend:
head:
[ C 0 ] SEQUENCE {
      [ U 2 ] INTEGER {
            00
      }
      [ U 2 ] INTEGER {
```

```
                    00
        }
    }
    item:
    [ U 2 ] INTEGER {
          00
    }
    result:
    [ C 0 ] SEQUENCE {
          [ U 2 ] INTEGER {
                    00
          }
          [ U 2 ] INTEGER {
                    00
          }
          [ U 2 ] INTEGER {
                    00
          }
    }
    asnAppend:
    head:
    [ C 0 ] SEQUENCE {
          [ U 2 ] INTEGER {
                    00
          }
          [ U 2 ] INTEGER {
                    00
          }
          [ U 2 ] INTEGER {
                    00
          }
    }
    item:
    [ U 16 ] SEQUENCE {
          [ U 16 ] SEQUENCE {
                [ U 6 ] OBJECTIDENTIFIER {
                        90 49
                }
                [ U 4 ] OCTETSTRING {

                }
          }
    }
    result:
    [ C 0 ] SEQUENCE {
          [ U 2 ] INTEGER {
                    00
          }
          [ U 2 ] INTEGER {
                    00
          }
```

```
        [ U 2 ] INTEGER {
                00
        }
        [ U 16 ] SEQUENCE {
                [ U 16 ] SEQUENCE {
                        [ U 6 ] OBJECTIDENTIFIER {
                                90 49
                        }
                        [ U 4 ] OCTETSTRING {

                        }
                }
        }
}
result: 00011738
smpSend:
asnAppend:
head:
[ U 16 ] SEQUENCE {
}
item:
[ U 2 ] INTEGER {
        00
}
result:
[ U 16 ] SEQUENCE {
        [ U 2 ] INTEGER {
                00
        }
}
asnAppend:
head:
[ U 16 ] SEQUENCE {
        [ U 2 ] INTEGER {
                00
        }
}
item:
[ U 4 ] OCTETSTRING {
        70 75 62 6C 69 63
}
result:
[ U 16 ] SEQUENCE {
        [ U 2 ] INTEGER {
                00
        }
        [ U 4 ] OCTETSTRING {
                70 75 62 6C 69 63
        }
}
asnAppend:
```

```
head:
[ U 16 ] SEQUENCE {
      [ U 2 ] INTEGER {
             00
      }
      [ U 4 ] OCTETSTRING {
             70 75 62 6C 69 63
      }
}
item:
[ C 0 ] SEQUENCE {
      [ U 2 ] INTEGER {
             00
      }
      [ U 2 ] INTEGER {
             00
      }
      [ U 2 ] INTEGER {
             00
      }
      [ U 16 ] SEQUENCE {
             [ U 16 ] SEQUENCE {
                    [ U 6 ] OBJECTIDENTIFIER {
                           90 49
                    }
                    [ U 4 ] OCTETSTRING {

                    }
             }
      }
}
result:
[ U 16 ] SEQUENCE {
      [ U 2 ] INTEGER {
             00
      }
      [ U 4 ] OCTETSTRING {
             70 75 62 6C 69 63
      }
      [ C 0 ] SEQUENCE {
             [ U 2 ] INTEGER {
                    00
             }
             [ U 2 ] INTEGER {
                    00
             }
             [ U 2 ] INTEGER {
                    00
             }
             [ U 16 ] SEQUENCE {
                    [ U 16 ] SEQUENCE {
```

```
                                  [ U 6 ] OBJECTIDENTIFIER {
                                          90 49
                                  }
                                  [ U 4 ] OCTETSTRING {

                                  }
                          }
                  }
          }
}
[ U 16 ] SEQUENCE {
      [ U 2 ] INTEGER {
              00
      }
      [ U 4 ] OCTETSTRING {
              70 75 62 6C 69 63
      }
      [ C 0 ] SEQUENCE {
              [ U 2 ] INTEGER {
                      00
              }
              [ U 2 ] INTEGER {
                      00
              }
              [ U 2 ] INTEGER {
                      00
              }
              [ U 16 ] SEQUENCE {
                      [ U 16 ] SEQUENCE {
                              [ U 6 ] OBJECTIDENTIFIER {
                                      90 49
                              }
                              [ U 4 ] OCTETSTRING {

                              }
                      }
              }
      }
}

30 20 02 01 00 04 06 70 75 62 6C 69 63 A0 13 02 01 00 02 01 00 02 01 00 30 08
30 06 06 02 90 49 04 00
udpSend:
30 20 02 01 00 04 06 70 75 62 6C 69 63 A0 13 02 01 00 02 01 00 02 01 00 30 08
30 06 06 02 90 49 04 00
30 20 02 01 00 04 06 70 75 62 6C 69 63 A2 13 02 01 00 02 01 02 02 01 01 30 08
30 06 06 02 90 49 04 00
asnNew dp 106A0
asnType0
asnType0 dp 106A0 np A708
aslChoice 1
```

```
asnLen0 asnLenVerify Max -1 Tot 2 Len 32 Min 20 4 4
asnSeq 4
asnPush
asnType0
asnType0 dp 10678 np A728
aslChoice 1
asnLen0 asnLenVerify Max 32 Tot 2 Len 1 Min 1 4 4
asnInteger0: 00
asnInteger1: 00
asnInteger0: 4
asnInteger0: 00010678
asnInteger1: 00
asnInteger0: 2
asnInteger1: 100
asnInteger1: 00
asnInteger1: 4
asnInteger1: 00010678
asnInteger1: 1
asnPop
asnSeq 4
asnPush
asnType0
asnType0 dp 10650 np A748
aslChoice 1
asnLen0 asnLenVerify Max 29 Tot 2 Len 6 Min 0 4 4
asnInteger2: 2
asnInteger2: 2
asnInteger2: 2
asnInteger2: 2
asnInteger2: 2
asnInteger2: 1
asnPop
asnSeq 4
asnPush
asnType0
asnType0 dp 10628 np A768
aslChoice 1
asnLen0 asnLenVerify Max 21 Tot 2 Len 19 Min 12 4 4
asnSeq 4
asnPush
asnType0
asnType0 dp 10600 np A7C8
aslChoice 1
asnLen0 asnLenVerify Max 19 Tot 2 Len 1 Min 1 4 4
asnInteger0: 00
asnInteger1: 00
asnInteger0: 17
asnInteger0: 00010600
asnInteger1: 00
asnInteger0: 2
asnInteger1: 100
```

```
asnInteger1: 00
asnInteger1: 17
asnInteger1: 00010600
asnInteger1: 1
asnPop
asnSeq 4
asnPush
asnType0
asnType0 dp 105D8 np A7E8
aslChoice 1
asnLen0 asnLenVerify Max 16 Tot 2 Len 1 Min 1 4 4
asnInteger0: 02
asnInteger1: 02
asnInteger0: 20
asnInteger0: 000105D8
asnInteger1: 02
asnInteger0: 2
asnInteger1: 100
asnInteger1: 02
asnInteger1: 20
asnInteger1: 000105D8
asnInteger1: 1
asnPop
asnSeq 4
asnPush
asnType0
asnType0 dp 105B0 np A808
aslChoice 1
asnLen0 asnLenVerify Max 13 Tot 2 Len 1 Min 1 4 4
asnInteger0: 01
asnInteger1: 01
asnInteger0: 23
asnInteger0: 000105B0
asnInteger1: 01
asnInteger0: 2
asnInteger1: 100
asnInteger1: 01
asnInteger1: 23
asnInteger1: 000105B0
asnInteger1: 1
asnPop
asnSeq 4
asnPush
asnType0
asnType0 dp 10588 np A828
aslChoice 1
asnLen0 asnLenVerify Max 10 Tot 2 Len 8 Min 0 4 4
asnSeqOf
asnPush
asnType0
asnType0 dp 10560 np A848
```

```
aslChoice 1
asnLen0 asnLenVerify Max 8 Tot 2 Len 6 Min 4 4 4
asnSeq 4
asnPush
asnType0
asnType0 dp 10538 np A868
aslChoice 1
asnLen0 asnLenVerify Max 6 Tot 2 Len 2 Min 0 4 4
asnObjectId0 1
asnObjectId1 2
asnObjectId1 49 1
asnPop
asnSeq 4
asnPush
asnType0
asnType0 dp 10510 np A888
aslChoice 1
asnLen0 asnLenVerify Max 2 Tot 2 Len 0 Min 0 4 4
asnPop
asnSeq 2
asnPop
asnSeqOf
asnPop
asnSeq 2
asnPop
asnSeq 2
asnPop
asnDecode bytesLeft 3686
smpInputEvent [ C 2 ] SEQUENCE {
        [ U 2 ] INTEGER {
                00
        }
        [ U 2 ] INTEGER {
                02
        }
        [ U 2 ] INTEGER {
                01
        }
        [ U 16 ] SEQUENCE OF {
                [ U 16 ] SEQUENCE {
                        [ U 6 ] OBJECTIDENTIFIER {
                                90 49
                        }
                        [ U 4 ] OCTETSTRING {

                        }
                }
        }
}
Request Id: 0
Error: noSuchName
```

```
Index: 1
Count: 1

Name: 53.1
Kind: OctetString
smxValueToText: Kind 2 Len 0
Value: ""

4
result: 0
```

APPENDIX E

DEBUG Output From Agent

```
NIL
systmInit: Hostid 1426085885
rteInit: rteHashSize 8
asnNew dp 12728
asnType0
asnType0 dp 12728 np C7F8
aslChoice 1
asnLen0 asnLenVerify Max -1 Tot 2 Len 33 Min 20 4 4
asnSeq 4
asnPush
asnType0
asnType0 dp 12700 np C818
aslChoice 1
asnLen0 asnLenVerify Max 33 Tot 2 Len 1 Min 1 4 4
asnInteger0: 00
asnInteger1: 00
asnInteger0: 4
asnInteger0: 00012700
asnInteger1: 00
asnInteger0: 2
asnInteger1: 100
asnInteger1: 00
asnInteger1: 4
asnInteger1: 00012700
asnInteger1: 1
asnPop
asnSeq 4
asnPush
asnType0
asnType0 dp 126D8 np C838
aslChoice 1
asnLen0 asnLenVerify Max 30 Tot 2 Len 6 Min 0 4 4
```

```
asnInteger2: 2
asnInteger2: 2
asnInteger2: 2
asnInteger2: 2
asnInteger2: 2
asnInteger2: 1
asnPop
asnSeq 4
asnPush
asnType0
asnType0 dp 126B0 np C858
aslChoice 1
asnLen0 asnLenVerify Max 22 Tot 2 Len 20 Min 12 4 4
asnSeq 4
asnPush
asnType0
asnType0 dp 12688 np C8B8
aslChoice 1
asnLen0 asnLenVerify Max 20 Tot 2 Len 1 Min 1 4 4
asnInteger0: 00
asnInteger1: 00
asnInteger0: 17
asnInteger0: 00012688
asnInteger1: 00
asnInteger0: 2
asnInteger1: 100
asnInteger1: 00
asnInteger1: 17
asnInteger1: 00012688
asnInteger1: 1
asnPop
asnSeq 4
asnPush
asnType0
asnType0 dp 12660 np C8D8
aslChoice 1
asnLen0 asnLenVerify Max 17 Tot 2 Len 1 Min 1 4 4
asnInteger0: 00
asnInteger1: 00
asnInteger0: 20
asnInteger0: 00012660
asnInteger1: 00
asnInteger0: 2
asnInteger1: 100
asnInteger1: 00
asnInteger1: 20
asnInteger1: 00012660
asnInteger1: 1
asnPop
asnSeq 4
asnPush
```

```
asnType0
asnType0 dp 12638 np C8F8
aslChoice 1
asnLen0 asnLenVerify Max 14 Tot 2 Len 1 Min 1 4 4
asnInteger0: 00
asnInteger1: 00
asnInteger0: 23
asnInteger0: 00012638
asnInteger1: 00
asnInteger0: 2
asnInteger1: 100
asnInteger1: 00
asnInteger1: 23
asnInteger1: 00012638
asnInteger1: 1
asnPop
asnSeq 4
asnPush
asnType0
asnType0 dp 12610 np C918
aslChoice 1
asnLen0 asnLenVerify Max 11 Tot 2 Len 9 Min 0 4 4
asnSeqOf
asnPush
asnType0
asnType0 dp 125E8 np C938
aslChoice 1
asnLen0 asnLenVerify Max 9 Tot 2 Len 7 Min 4 4 4
asnSeq 4
asnPush
asnType0
asnType0 dp 125C0 np C958
aslChoice 1
asnLen0 asnLenVerify Max 7 Tot 2 Len 3 Min 0 4 4
asnObjectId0 1
asnObjectId1 2
asnObjectId1 2
asnObjectId1 02 1
asnPop
asnSeq 4
asnPush
asnType0
asnType0 dp 12598 np C978
aslChoice 1
asnLen0 asnLenVerify Max 2 Tot 2 Len 0 Min 0 4 4
asnPop
asnSeq 2
asnPop
asnSeqOf
asnPop
asnSeq 2
```

```
asnPop
asnSeq 2
asnPop
asnDecode bytesLeft 3685
smpInputEvent [ C 0 ] SEQUENCE {
        [ U 2 ] INTEGER {
                00
        }
        [ U 2 ] INTEGER {
                00
        }
        [ U 2 ] INTEGER {
                00
        }
        [ U 16 ] SEQUENCE OF {
                [ U 16 ] SEQUENCE {
                        [ U 6 ] OBJECTIDENTIFIER {
                                93 59 02
                        }
                        [ U 4 ] OCTETSTRING {

                        }
                }
        }
}
smpGetOp
smpGetOp: asn:
[ C 0 ] SEQUENCE {
        [ U 2 ] INTEGER {
                00
        }
        [ U 2 ] INTEGER {
                00
        }
        [ U 2 ] INTEGER {
                00
        }
        [ U 16 ] SEQUENCE OF {
                [ U 16 ] SEQUENCE {
                        [ U 6 ] OBJECTIDENTIFIER {
                                93 59 02
                        }
                        [ U 4 ] OCTETSTRING {

                        }
                }
        }
}
smpGetOp: seq:
[ U 16 ] SEQUENCE OF {
        [ U 16 ] SEQUENCE {
```

```
            [ U 6 ] OBJECTIDENTIFIER {
                    93 59 02
            }
            [ U 4 ] OCTETSTRING {

            }
      }
}
smpGetOp: bind:
[ U 16 ] SEQUENCE {
      [ U 6 ] OBJECTIDENTIFIER {
              93 59 02
      }
      [ U 4 ] OCTETSTRING {

      }
}
smpGetOp: name:
[ U 6 ] OBJECTIDENTIFIER {
        93 59 02
}
smpGetOp 1
smpGetOp: error 2
smpGetOp: rseq:
[ U 16 ] SEQUENCE OF {
}
smpReply:
asnAppend:
head:
[ C 2 ] SEQUENCE {
}
item:
[ U 2 ] INTEGER {
        00
}
result:
[ C 2 ] SEQUENCE {
      [ U 2 ] INTEGER {
              00
      }
}
asnAppend:
head:
[ C 2 ] SEQUENCE {
      [ U 2 ] INTEGER {
              00
      }
}
item:
[ U 2 ] INTEGER {
        02
```

```
        }
        result:
        [ C 2 ] SEQUENCE {
              [ U 2 ] INTEGER {
                      00
              }
              [ U 2 ] INTEGER {
                      02
              }
        }
        asnAppend:
        head:
        [ C 2 ] SEQUENCE {
              [ U 2 ] INTEGER {
                      00
              }
              [ U 2 ] INTEGER {
                      02
              }
        }
        item:
        [ U 2 ] INTEGER {
              01
        }
        result:
        [ C 2 ] SEQUENCE {
              [ U 2 ] INTEGER {
                      00
              }
              [ U 2 ] INTEGER {
                      02
              }
              [ U 2 ] INTEGER {
                      01
              }
        }
        asnAppend:
        head:
        [ C 2 ] SEQUENCE {
              [ U 2 ] INTEGER {
                      00
              }
              [ U 2 ] INTEGER {
                      02
              }
              [ U 2 ] INTEGER {
                      01
              }
        }
        item:
        [ U 16 ] SEQUENCE OF {
```

```
        [ U 16 ] SEQUENCE {
                [ U 6 ] OBJECTIDENTIFIER {
                        93 59 02
                }
                [ U 4 ] OCTETSTRING {

                }
        }
}
result:
[ C 2 ] SEQUENCE {
        [ U 2 ] INTEGER {
                00
        }
        [ U 2 ] INTEGER {
                02
        }
        [ U 2 ] INTEGER {
                01
        }
        [ U 16 ] SEQUENCE OF {
                [ U 16 ] SEQUENCE {
                        [ U 6 ] OBJECTIDENTIFIER {
                                93 59 02
                        }
                        [ U 4 ] OCTETSTRING {

                        }
                }
        }
}
smpSend:
asnAppend:
head:
[ U 16 ] SEQUENCE {
}
item:
[ U 2 ] INTEGER {
        00
}
result:
[ U 16 ] SEQUENCE {
        [ U 2 ] INTEGER {
                00
        }
}
asnAppend:
head:
[ U 16 ] SEQUENCE {
        [ U 2 ] INTEGER {
                00
```

```
              }
          }
          item:
          [ U 4 ] OCTETSTRING {
                70 75 62 6C 69 63
          }
          result:
          [ U 16 ] SEQUENCE {
                [ U 2 ] INTEGER {
                      00
                }
                [ U 4 ] OCTETSTRING {
                      70 75 62 6C 69 63
                }
          }
          asnAppend:
          head:
          [ U 16 ] SEQUENCE {
                [ U 2 ] INTEGER {
                      00
                }
                [ U 4 ] OCTETSTRING {
                      70 75 62 6C 69 63
                }
          }
          item:
          [ C 2 ] SEQUENCE {
                [ U 2 ] INTEGER {
                      00
                }
                [ U 2 ] INTEGER {
                      02
                }
                [ U 2 ] INTEGER {
                      01
                }
                [ U 16 ] SEQUENCE OF {
                      [ U 16 ] SEQUENCE {
                            [ U 6 ] OBJECTIDENTIFIER {
                                  93 59 02
                            }
                            [ U 4 ] OCTETSTRING {

                            }
                      }
                }
          }
          result:
          [ U 16 ] SEQUENCE {
                [ U 2 ] INTEGER {
                      00
```

```
        }
        [ U 4 ] OCTETSTRING {
                70 75 62 6C 69 63
        }
        [ C 2 ] SEQUENCE {
                [ U 2 ] INTEGER {
                        00
                }
                [ U 2 ] INTEGER {
                        02
                }
                [ U 2 ] INTEGER {
                        01
                }
                [ U 16 ] SEQUENCE OF {
                        [ U 16 ] SEQUENCE {
                                [ U 6 ] OBJECTIDENTIFIER {
                                        93 59 02
                                }
                                [ U 4 ] OCTETSTRING {

                                }
                        }
                }
        }
}
[ U 16 ] SEQUENCE {
        [ U 2 ] INTEGER {
                00
        }
        [ U 4 ] OCTETSTRING {
                70 75 62 6C 69 63
        }
        [ C 2 ] SEQUENCE {
                [ U 2 ] INTEGER {
                        00
                }
                [ U 2 ] INTEGER {
                        02
                }
                [ U 2 ] INTEGER {
                        01
                }
                [ U 16 ] SEQUENCE OF {
                        [ U 16 ] SEQUENCE {
                                [ U 6 ] OBJECTIDENTIFIER {
                                        93 59 02
                                }
                                [ U 4 ] OCTETSTRING {

                                }
```

```
                        }
                  }
            }
      }

30 21 02 01 00 04 06 70 75 62 6C 69 63 A2 14 02 01 00 02 01 02 02 01 01 30 09
30 07 06 03 93 59 02 04 00
udpSend:
30 21 02 01 00 04 06 70 75 62 6C 69 63 A2 14 02 01 00 02 01 02 02 01 01 30 09
30 07 06 03 93 59 02 04 00
4
```

APPENDIX F

Basic SMI/MIB Example

```
mgmt          OBJECT IDENTIFIER ::= { iso org(3) dod(6) internet(1) mgmt(2) }
mib           OBJECT IDENTIFIER ::= { mgmt 1 }
directory     OBJECT IDENTIFIER ::= { internet 1 }
experimental  OBJECT IDENTIFIER ::= { internet 3 }
private       OBJECT IDENTIFIER ::= { internet 4 }
enterprises   OBJECT IDENTIFIER ::= { private 1 }

system        OBJECT IDENTIFIER ::= { mib 1 }
interfaces    OBJECT IDENTIFIER ::= { mib 2 }
at            OBJECT IDENTIFIER ::= { mib 3 }
ip            OBJECT IDENTIFIER ::= { mib 4 }
icmp          OBJECT IDENTIFIER ::= { mib 5 }
tcp           OBJECT IDENTIFIER ::= { mib 6 }
udp           OBJECT IDENTIFIER ::= { mib 7 }
egp           OBJECT IDENTIFIER ::= { mib 8 }

— object types

— the System group

sysDescr OBJECT-TYPE
    SYNTAX   OCTET STRING
    ACCESS   read-only
    STATUS   mandatory
    ::= { system 1 }

sysObjectID OBJECT-TYPE
    SYNTAX   OBJECT IDENTIFIER
    ACCESS   read-only
    STATUS   mandatory
    ::= { system 2 }
```

```
sysUpTime OBJECT-TYPE
    SYNTAX   TimeTicks
    ACCESS   read-only
    STATUS   mandatory
    ::= { system 3 }

- the Interfaces group

ifNumber OBJECT-TYPE
    SYNTAX   INTEGER
    ACCESS   read-only
    STATUS   mandatory
    ::= { interfaces 1 }

- the Interfaces table

ifTable OBJECT-TYPE
    SYNTAX   SEQUENCE OF IfEntry
    ACCESS   read-write
    STATUS   mandatory
    ::= { interfaces 2 }

ifEntry OBJECT-TYPE
    SYNTAX   IfEntry
    ACCESS   read-write
    STATUS   mandatory
    ::= { ifTable 1 }

IfEntry ::= SEQUENCE {
    ifIndex
        INTEGER,
    ifDescr
        OCTET STRING,
    ifType
        INTEGER,
    ifMtu
        INTEGER,
    ifSpeed
        Gauge,
    ifPhysAddress
        OCTET STRING,
    ifAdminStatus
        INTEGER,
    ifOperStatus
        INTEGER,
    ifLastChange
        TimeTicks,
    ifInOctets
        Counter,
    ifInUcastPkts
        Counter,
```

```
        ifInNUcastPkts
          Counter,
        ifInDiscards
          Counter,
        ifInErrors
          Counter,
        ifInUnknownProtos
          Counter,
        ifOutOctets
          Counter,
        ifOutUcastPkts
          Counter,
        ifOutNUcastPkts
          Counter,
        ifOutDiscards
          Counter,
        ifOutErrors
          Counter,
        ifOutQLen
          Gauge
}

ifIndex OBJECT-TYPE
    SYNTAX  INTEGER
    ACCESS  read-only
    STATUS  mandatory
    ::= { ifEntry 1 }

ifDescr OBJECT-TYPE
    SYNTAX  OCTET STRING
    ACCESS  read-only
    STATUS  mandatory
    ::= { ifEntry 2 }

ifType OBJECT-TYPE
    SYNTAX  INTEGER {
        other(1),        — none of the following
        regular1822(2),
        hdh1822(3),
        ddn-x25(4),
        rfc877-x25(5),
        ethernet-csmacd(6),
        iso88023-csmacd(7),
        iso88024-tokenBus(8),
        iso88025-tokenRing(9),
        iso88026-man(10),
        starLan(11),
        proteon-10MBit(12),
        proteon-80MBit(13),
        hyperchannel(14),
        fddi(15),
```

```
            lapb(16),
            sdlc(17),
            t1-carrier(18),
            cept(19),
            basicIsdn(20),
            primaryIsdn(21),
                        - proprietary serial
            propPointToPointSerial(22)
        }
    ACCESS  read-only
    STATUS  mandatory
    ::= { ifEntry 3 }

ifMtu OBJECT-TYPE
    SYNTAX  INTEGER
    ACCESS  read-only
    STATUS  mandatory
    ::= { ifEntry 4 }

    ifSpeed OBJECT-TYPE
      SYNTAX  Gauge
      ACCESS  read-only
      STATUS  mandatory
      ::= { ifEntry 5 }

    ifPhysAddress OBJECT-TYPE
      SYNTAX  OCTET STRING
      ACCESS  read-only
      STATUS  mandatory
      ::= { ifEntry 6 }

    ifAdminStatus OBJECT-TYPE
      SYNTAX  INTEGER {
          up(1),        - ready to pass packets
          down(2),
          testing(3)    - in some test mode
                              }
      ACCESS  read-write
      STATUS  mandatory
      ::= { ifEntry 7 }

    ifOperStatus OBJECT-TYPE
      SYNTAX  INTEGER {
          up(1),        - ready to pass packets
          down(2),
          testing(3)    - in some test mode
          }
      ACCESS  read-only
      STATUS  mandatory
      ::= { ifEntry 8 }
```

```
ifLastChange OBJECT-TYPE
  SYNTAX   TimeTicks
  ACCESS   read-only
  STATUS   mandatory
  ::= { ifEntry 9 }

ifInOctets OBJECT-TYPE
  SYNTAX   Counter
  ACCESS   read-only
 ·STATUS   mandatory
  ::= { ifEntry 10 }

ifInUcastPkts OBJECT-TYPE
  SYNTAX   Counter
  ACCESS   read-only
  STATUS   mandatory
  ::=   { ifEntry 11 }

ifInNUcastPkts OBJECT-TYPE
  SYNTAX   Counter
  ACCESS   read-only
  STATUS   mandatory
  ::= { ifEntry 12 }

ifInDiscards OBJECT-TYPE
  SYNTAX   Counter
  ACCESS   read-only
  STATUS   mandatory
  ::= { ifEntry 13 }

ifInErrors OBJECT-TYPE
  SYNTAX   Counter
  ACCESS   read-only
  STATUS   mandatory
  ::= { ifEntry 14 }

ifInUnknownProtos OBJECT-TYPE
  SYNTAX   Counter
  ACCESS   read-only
  STATUS   mandatory
  ::= { ifEntry 15 }

ifOutOctets OBJECT-TYPE
  SYNTAX   Counter
  ACCESS   read-only
  STATUS   mandatory
  ::= { ifEntry 16 }

ifOutUcastPkts OBJECT-TYPE
  SYNTAX   Counter
  ACCESS   read-only
```

```
        STATUS  mandatory
        ::= { ifEntry 17 }

    ifOutNUcastPkts OBJECT-TYPE
        SYNTAX  Counter
        ACCESS  read-only
        STATUS  mandatory
        ::= { ifEntry 18 }

    ifOutDiscards OBJECT-TYPE
        SYNTAX  Counter
        ACCESS  read-only
        STATUS  mandatory
        ::= { ifEntry 19 }

        ifOutErrors OBJECT-TYPE
        SYNTAX  Counter
        ACCESS  read-only
        STATUS  mandatory
        ::= { ifEntry 20 }

    ifOutQLen OBJECT-TYPE
        SYNTAX  Gauge
        ACCESS  read-only
        STATUS  mandatory
        ::= { ifEntry 21 }

    - the Address Translation group

    atTable OBJECT-TYPE
        SYNTAX  SEQUENCE OF AtEntry
        ACCESS  read-write
        STATUS  mandatory
        ::= { at 1 }

    atEntry OBJECT-TYPE
        SYNTAX  AtEntry
        ACCESS  read-write
        STATUS  mandatory
        ::= { atTable 1 }

    AtEntry ::= SEQUENCE {
        atIfIndex
            INTEGER,
        atPhysAddress
            OCTET STRING,
        atNetAddress
            NetworkAddress
    }
```

```
atIfIndex OBJECT-TYPE
  SYNTAX  INTEGER
  ACCESS  read-write
  STATUS  mandatory
  ::= { atEntry 1 }

atPhysAddress OBJECT-TYPE
  SYNTAX  OCTET STRING
  ACCESS  read-write
  STATUS  mandatory
  ::= { atEntry 2 }

atNetAddress OBJECT-TYPE
  SYNTAX  NetworkAddress
  ACCESS  read-write
  STATUS  mandatory
  ::= { atEntry 3 }

— the IP group

ipForwarding OBJECT-TYPE
  SYNTAX  INTEGER {
  gateway(1), — entity forwards datagrams
  host(2)    — entity does NOT forward datagrams
    }
  ACCESS  read-only
  STATUS  mandatory
  ::= { ip 1 }

ipDefaultTTL OBJECT-TYPE
  SYNTAX  INTEGER
  ACCESS  read-write
  STATUS  mandatory
  ::= { ip 2 }

ipInReceives OBJECT-TYPE
  SYNTAX  Counter
  ACCESS  read-only
  STATUS  mandatory
  ::= { ip 3 }

ipInHdrErrors OBJECT-TYPE
  SYNTAX  Counter
  ACCESS  read-only
  STATUS  mandatory
  ::= { ip 4 }

ipInAddrErrors OBJECT-TYPE
  SYNTAX  Counter
  ACCESS  read-only
  STATUS  mandatory
```

```
      ::= { ip 5 }

ipForwDatagrams OBJECT-TYPE
  SYNTAX  Counter
  ACCESS  read-only
  STATUS  mandatory
  ::= { ip 6 }

ipInUnknownProtos OBJECT-TYPE
  SYNTAX  Counter
  ACCESS  read-only
  STATUS  mandatory
  ::= { ip 7 }

ipInDiscards OBJECT-TYPE
  SYNTAX  Counter
  ACCESS  read-only
  STATUS  mandatory
  ::= { ip 8 }

ipInDelivers OBJECT-TYPE
  SYNTAX  Counter
  ACCESS  read-only
  STATUS  mandatory
  ::= { ip 9 }

ipOutRequests OBJECT-TYPE
  SYNTAX  Counter
  ACCESS  read-only
  STATUS  mandatory
  ::= { ip 10 }

ipOutDiscards OBJECT-TYPE
  SYNTAX  Counter
  ACCESS  read-only
  STATUS  mandatory
  ::= { ip 11 }

ipOutNoRoutes OBJECT-TYPE
  SYNTAX  Counter
  ACCESS  read-only
  STATUS  mandatory
  ::= { ip 12 }

ipReasmTimeout OBJECT-TYPE
  SYNTAX  INTEGER
  ACCESS  read-only
  STATUS  mandatory
  ::= { ip 13 }
```

```
ipReasmReqds OBJECT-TYPE
  SYNTAX  Counter
  ACCESS  read-only
  STATUS  mandatory
  ::= { ip 14 }

ipReasmOKs OBJECT-TYPE
  SYNTAX  Counter
  ACCESS  read-only
  STATUS  mandatory
  ::= { ip 15 }

ipReasmFails OBJECT-TYPE
  SYNTAX  Counter
  ACCESS  read-only
  STATUS  mandatory
  ::= { ip 16 }

ipFragOKs OBJECT-TYPE
  SYNTAX  Counter
  ACCESS  read-only
  STATUS  mandatory
  ::= { ip 17 }

ipFragFails OBJECT-TYPE
  SYNTAX  Counter
  ACCESS  read-only
  STATUS  mandatory
  ::= { ip 18 }

ipFragCreates OBJECT-TYPE
  SYNTAX  Counter
  ACCESS  read-only
  STATUS  mandatory
  ::= { ip 19 }

- the IP Interface table

ipAddrTable OBJECT-TYPE
  SYNTAX  SEQUENCE OF IpAddrEntry
  ACCESS  read-only
  STATUS  mandatory
  ::= { ip 20 }

ipAddrEntry OBJECT-TYPE
  SYNTAX  IpAddrEntry
  ACCESS  read-only
  STATUS  mandatory
  ::= { ipAddrTable 1 }
```

```
IpAddrEntry ::= SEQUENCE {
  ipAdEntAddr
    IpAddress,
  ipAdEntIfIndex
    INTEGER,
  ipAdEntNetMask
    IpAddress,
  ipAdEntBcastAddr
    INTEGER
}

ipAdEntAddr OBJECT-TYPE
  SYNTAX  IpAddress
  ACCESS  read-only
  STATUS  mandatory
  ::=  { ipAddrEntry 1 }

ipAdEntIfIndex OBJECT-TYPE
  SYNTAX  INTEGER
  ACCESS  read-only
  STATUS  mandatory
  ::=  { ipAddrEntry 2 }

ipAdEntNetMask OBJECT-TYPE
  SYNTAX  IpAddress
  ACCESS  read-only
  STATUS  mandatory
  ::=  { ipAddrEntry 3 }

ipAdEntBcastAddr OBJECT-TYPE
  SYNTAX  INTEGER
  ACCESS  read-only
  STATUS  mandatory
  ::= { ipAddrEntry 4 }

- the IP Routing table

ipRoutingTable OBJECT-TYPE
  SYNTAX  SEQUENCE OF IpRouteEntry
  ACCESS  read-write
  STATUS  mandatory
  ::= { ip 21 }

ipRouteEntry OBJECT-TYPE
  SYNTAX  IpRouteEntry
  ACCESS  read-write
  STATUS  mandatory
  ::= { ipRoutingTable 1 }
```

```
IpRouteEntry ::= SEQUENCE {
  ipRouteDest
     IpAddress,
  ipRouteIfIndex
     INTEGER,
  ipRouteMetric1
     INTEGER,
  ipRouteMetric2
     INTEGER,
  ipRouteMetric3
     INTEGER,
  ipRouteMetric4
     INTEGER,
  ipRouteNextHop
     IpAddress,
  ipRouteType
     INTEGER,
  ipRouteProto
     INTEGER,
  ipRouteAge
     INTEGER
}

ipRouteDest OBJECT-TYPE
  SYNTAX  IpAddress
  ACCESS  read-write
  STATUS  mandatory
  ::= { ipRouteEntry 1 }

ipRouteIfIndex  OBJECT-TYPE
  SYNTAX  INTEGER
  ACCESS  read-write
  STATUS  mandatory
  ::= { ipRouteEntry 2 }

ipRouteMetric1 OBJECT-TYPE
  SYNTAX  INTEGER
  ACCESS  read-write
  STATUS  mandatory
  ::= { ipRouteEntry 3 }

ipRouteMetric2 OBJECT-TYPE
  SYNTAX  INTEGER
  ACCESS  read-write
  STATUS  mandatory
  ::= { ipRouteEntry 4 }

ipRouteMetric3 OBJECT-TYPE
  SYNTAX  INTEGER
  ACCESS  read-write
  STATUS  mandatory
  ::= { ipRouteEntry 5 }
```

```
ipRouteMetric4 OBJECT-TYPE
  SYNTAX  INTEGER
  ACCESS  read-write
  STATUS  mandatory
  ::= { ipRouteEntry 6 }

ipRouteNextHop OBJECT-TYPE
  SYNTAX  IpAddress
  ACCESS  read-write
  STATUS  mandatory
  ::= { ipRouteEntry 7 }

ipRouteType OBJECT-TYPE
  SYNTAX  INTEGER {
  other(1),        — none of the following

  invalid(2),      — an invalidated route

                   — route to directly
  direct(3),       — connected (sub-)network

                   — route to a non-local
   remote(4),      — host/network/sub-network
   }
  ACCESS  read-write
  STATUS  mandatory
  ::= { ipRouteEntry 8 }

ipRouteProto OBJECT-TYPE
  SYNTAX  INTEGER {
  other(1),        — none of the following

                   — non-protocol information
                   —   e.g., manually
  local(2),        —   configured entries

                   — set via a network
  netmgmt(3),      —   management protocol

                   — obtained via ICMP,
  icmp(4),         —   e.g., Redirect

                   — the following are
                   — gateway routing protocols
  egp(5),
  ggp(6),
  hello(7),
  rip(8),
  is-is(9),
  es-is(10),
```

```
    ciscoIgrp(11),
    bbnSpfIgp(12),
    oigp(13)
      }
  ACCESS  read-only
  STATUS  mandatory
  ::= { ipRouteEntry 9 }

ipRouteAge OBJECT-TYPE
  SYNTAX  INTEGER
  ACCESS  read-write
  STATUS  mandatory
  ::= { ipRouteEntry 10 }

- the ICMP group

icmpInMsgs OBJECT-TYPE
  SYNTAX  Counter
  ACCESS  read-only
  STATUS  mandatory
  ::= { icmp 1 }

icmpInErrors OBJECT-TYPE
  SYNTAX  Counter
  ACCESS  read-only
  STATUS  mandatory
  ::= { icmp 2 }

icmpInDestUnreachs OBJECT-TYPE
  SYNTAX  Counter

  ACCESS  read-only
  STATUS  mandatory
  ::= { icmp 3 }

icmpInTimeExcds OBJECT-TYPE
  SYNTAX  Counter
  ACCESS  read-only
  STATUS  mandatory
  ::= { icmp 4 }

icmpInParmProbs OBJECT-TYPE
  SYNTAX  Counter
  ACCESS  read-only
  STATUS  mandatory
  ::= { icmp 5 }

icmpInSrcQuenchs OBJECT-TYPE
  SYNTAX  Counter
  ACCESS  read-only
  STATUS  mandatory
  ::= { icmp 6 }
```

```
icmpInRedirects OBJECT-TYPE
  SYNTAX   Counter
  ACCESS   read-only
  STATUS   mandatory
  ::= { icmp 7 }

icmpInEchos OBJECT-TYPE
  SYNTAX   Counter
  ACCESS   read-only
  STATUS   mandatory
  ::= { icmp 8 }

icmpInEchoReps OBJECT-TYPE
  SYNTAX   Counter
  ACCESS   read-only
  STATUS   mandatory
  ::= { icmp 9 }

icmpInTimestamps OBJECT-TYPE
  SYNTAX   Counter
  ACCESS   read-only
  STATUS   mandatory
  ::= { icmp 10 }

icmpInTimestampReps OBJECT-TYPE
  SYNTAX   Counter
  ACCESS   read-only
  STATUS   mandatory
  ::= { icmp 11 }

icmpInAddrMasks OBJECT-TYPE
  SYNTAX   Counter
  ACCESS   read-only
  STATUS   mandatory
  ::= { icmp 12 }

icmpInAddrMaskReps OBJECT-TYPE
  SYNTAX   Counter
  ACCESS   read-only
  STATUS   mandatory
  ::= { icmp 13 }

icmpOutMsgs OBJECT-TYPE
  SYNTAX   Counter
  ACCESS   read-only
  STATUS   mandatory
  ::= { icmp 14 }

icmpOutErrors OBJECT-TYPE
```

```
   SYNTAX   Counter
   ACCESS   read-only
   STATUS   mandatory
   ::= { icmp 15 }

icmpOutDestUnreachs OBJECT-TYPE
   SYNTAX   Counter
   ACCESS   read-only
   STATUS   mandatory
   ::= { icmp 16 }

icmpOutTimeExcds OBJECT-TYPE
   SYNTAX   Counter
   ACCESS   read-only
   STATUS   mandatory
   ::= { icmp 17 }

icmpOutParmProbs OBJECT-TYPE
   SYNTAX   Counter
   ACCESS   read-only
   STATUS   mandatory
   ::= { icmp 18 }

icmpOutSrcQuenchs OBJECT-TYPE
   SYNTAX   Counter
   ACCESS   read-only
   STATUS   mandatory
   ::= { icmp 19 }

icmpOutRedirects OBJECT-TYPE
   SYNTAX   Counter
   ACCESS   read-only
   STATUS   mandatory
   ::= { icmp 20 }

icmpOutEchos OBJECT-TYPE
   SYNTAX   Counter
   ACCESS   read-only
   STATUS   mandatory
   ::= { icmp 21 }

icmpOutEchoReps OBJECT-TYPE
   SYNTAX   Counter
   ACCESS   read-only
   STATUS   mandatory
   ::= { icmp 22 }

icmpOutTimestamps OBJECT-TYPE
   SYNTAX   Counter
   ACCESS   read-only
   STATUS   mandatory
```

```
   ::= { icmp 23 }

icmpOutTimestampReps OBJECT-TYPE
   SYNTAX  Counter
   ACCESS  read-only
   STATUS  mandatory
   ::= { icmp 24 }

icmpOutAddrMasks OBJECT-TYPE
   SYNTAX  Counter
   ACCESS  read-only
   STATUS  mandatory
   ::= { icmp 25 }

icmpOutAddrMaskReps OBJECT-TYPE
   SYNTAX  Counter
   ACCESS  read-only
   STATUS  mandatory
   ::= { icmp 26 }

- the TCP group

tcpRtoAlgorithm OBJECT-TYPE
   SYNTAX  INTEGER {
   other(1),    - none of the following
   constant(2), - a constant rto
   rsre(3),     - MIL-STD-1778, Appendix B
   vanj(4)      - Van Jacobson's algorithm [11]
      }
   ACCESS  read-only
   STATUS  mandatory
   ::= { tcp 1 }

tcpRtoMin OBJECT-TYPE
   SYNTAX  INTEGER
   ACCESS  read-only
   STATUS  mandatory
   ::= { tcp 2 }

tcpRtoMax OBJECT-TYPE
   SYNTAX  INTEGER
   ACCESS  read-only
   STATUS  mandatory
   ::= { tcp 3 }

tcpMaxConn OBJECT-TYPE
   SYNTAX  INTEGER
   ACCESS  read-only
   STATUS  mandatory
   ::= { tcp 4 }
tcpActiveOpens OBJECT-TYPE
```

```
   SYNTAX   Counter
   ACCESS   read-only
   STATUS   mandatory
   ::= { tcp 5 }

tcpPassiveOpens OBJECT-TYPE
   SYNTAX   Counter
   ACCESS   read-only
   STATUS   mandatory
   ::= { tcp 6 }

tcpAttemptFails OBJECT-TYPE
   SYNTAX   Counter
   ACCESS   read-only
   STATUS   mandatory
   ::= { tcp 7 }

tcpEstabResets OBJECT-TYPE
   SYNTAX   Counter
   ACCESS   read-only
   STATUS   mandatory
   ::= { tcp 8 }

tcpCurrEstab OBJECT-TYPE
   SYNTAX   Gauge
   ACCESS   read-only
   STATUS   mandatory
   ::= { tcp 9 }

tcpInSegs OBJECT-TYPE
   SYNTAX   Counter
   ACCESS   read-only
   STATUS   mandatory
   ::= { tcp 10 }

tcpOutSegs OBJECT-TYPE
   SYNTAX   Counter
   ACCESS   read-only
   STATUS   mandatory
   ::= { tcp 11 }

tcpRetransSegs OBJECT-TYPE
   SYNTAX   Counter
   ACCESS   read-only
   STATUS   mandatory
   ::= { tcp 12 }

- the TCP connections table
```

```
tcpConnTable OBJECT-TYPE
  SYNTAX   SEQUENCE OF TcpConnEntry
  ACCESS   read-only
  STATUS   mandatory
  ::= { tcp 13 }

tcpConnEntry OBJECT-TYPE
  SYNTAX   TcpConnEntry
  ACCESS   read-only
  STATUS   mandatory
  ::= { tcpConnTable 1 }

TcpConnEntry ::= SEQUENCE {
  tcpConnState
      INTEGER,
  tcpConnLocalAddress
      IpAddress,
  tcpConnLocalPort
      INTEGER (0..65535),
  tcpConnRemAddress
      IpAddress,
  tcpConnRemPort
      INTEGER (0..65535)
}

tcpConnState OBJECT-TYPE
  SYNTAX   INTEGER {
      closed(1),
      listen(2),
      synSent(3),
      synReceived(4),
      established(5),
      finWait1(6),
      finWait2(7),
      closeWait(8),
      lastAck(9),
      closing(10),
      timeWait(11)
    }
  ACCESS   read-only
  STATUS   mandatory
  ::= { tcpConnEntry 1 }

tcpConnLocalAddress OBJECT-TYPE
  SYNTAX   IpAddress
  ACCESS   read-only
  STATUS   mandatory
  ::= { tcpConnEntry 2 }

tcpConnLocalPort OBJECT-TYPE
  SYNTAX   INTEGER (0..65535)
  ACCESS   read-only
```

```
        STATUS   mandatory
        ::= { tcpConnEntry 3 }

    tcpConnRemAddress OBJECT-TYPE
        SYNTAX   IpAddress
        ACCESS   read-only
        STATUS   mandatory
        ::= { tcpConnEntry 4 }

    tcpConnRemPort OBJECT-TYPE
        SYNTAX   INTEGER (0..65535)
        ACCESS   read-only
        STATUS   mandatory
        ::= { tcpConnEntry 5 }

    - the UDP group

    udpInDatagrams OBJECT-TYPE
        SYNTAX   Counter
        ACCESS   read-only
        STATUS   mandatory
        ::= { udp 1 }

    udpNoPorts OBJECT-TYPE
        SYNTAX   Counter
        ACCESS   read-only
        STATUS   mandatory
        ::= { udp 2 }

    udpInErrors OBJECT-TYPE
        SYNTAX   Counter
        ACCESS   read-only
        STATUS   mandatory
        ::= { udp 3 }

    udpOutDatagrams OBJECT-TYPE
        SYNTAX   Counter
        ACCESS   read-only
        STATUS   mandatory
        ::= { udp 4 }

    - the EGP group

    egpInMsgs OBJECT-TYPE
        SYNTAX   Counter
        ACCESS   read-only
        STATUS   mandatory
        ::= { egp 1 }

    egpInErrors OBJECT-TYPE
        SYNTAX   Counter
        ACCESS   read-only
```

```
        STATUS  mandatory
        ::= { egp 2 }

egpOutMsgs OBJECT-TYPE
    SYNTAX  Counter
    ACCESS  read-only
    STATUS  mandatory
    ::= { egp 3 }

egpOutErrors OBJECT-TYPE
    SYNTAX  Counter
    ACCESS  read-only
    STATUS  mandatory
    ::= { egp 4 }

— the EGP Neighbor table

egpNeighTable OBJECT-TYPE
    SYNTAX  SEQUENCE OF EgpNeighEntry
    ACCESS  read-only
    STATUS  mandatory
    ::= { egp 5 }

egpNeighEntry OBJECT-TYPE
    SYNTAX  EgpNeighEntry
    ACCESS  read-only
    STATUS  mandatory
    ::= { egpNeighTable 1 }

EgpNeighEntry ::= SEQUENCE {
    egpNeighState
        INTEGER,
    egpNeighAddr
        IpAddress
}

egpNeighState OBJECT-TYPE
    SYNTAX  INTEGER {
        idle(1),
        acquisition(2),
        down(3),
        up(4),
        cease(5)
        }
    ACCESS  read-only
    STATUS  mandatory
    ::= { egpNeighEntry 1 }

egpNeighAddr OBJECT-TYPE
    SYNTAX  IpAddress
    ACCESS  read-only
    STATUS  mandatory
    ::= { egpNeighEntry 2 }
```

Glossary

abstract syntax: a description of a data type that is independent of machine-oriented structures and restrictions.

Abstract Syntax Notation One: the OSI language for describing abstract syntax.

access mode: the level of authorization implied by an SNMP community.

ACK: short for acknowledgment.

acknowledgment: a response sent by a receiver to indicate successful reception of information.

active open: the sequence events that occur when an application entity directs the TCP software to establish a connection.

address class: a method used to determine the boundary between the network and host portions of an IP address.

address mask: a 32-bit quantity indicating which bits in an IP address refer to the network portion.

address resolution: a means for mapping network-layer addresses onto media-specific addresses.

Address Resolution Protocol: the protocol in the Internet suite of protocols used to map IP addresses onto the media address.

administrative framework: a scheme for defining a policy of authentication and authorization.

agent: the SNMP process running on the server end of the exchange. Serving variables to the client Network Management System.

American National Standards Institute: the U.S. national standards body. ANSI is a member of ISO.

ANSI: *see American National Standards Institute.*

AP: *see application process.*

API: *see Application Programmer's Interface.*

application layer: that portion of an OSI system ultimately responsible for managing communication between application processes (APs).

Applications Programmer Interface: a set of calling conventions defining how a service is called by a program or programmer.

ARP: *see Address Resolution Protocol.*

ARPA: Advanced Research Projects Agency now known as DARPA.

authentication entity: that portion of an SNMP agent responsible for verifying that an SNMP entity is a member of the community it claims to be in. This entity is also responsible for encoding/decoding SNMP messages according to the authentication algorithm of a given community.

ARPA: *see Defense Advanced Research Projects Agency.*

ASN.1: *see Abstract Syntax Notation One.*

B

baseband: network technology that uses a single carrier frequency and requires all stations attached to the network to participate.

baud: the number of times per second a signal can change on a transmission line. Transmission lines use two signals so baud rate equals the number of bits per second that can be transferred.

BER: *see Basic Encoding Rules.*

big endian: format with most-significant byte (bit) comes first.

BISYNC: BInary SYNchronous Communication—an early low-level protocol developed by IBM.

broadband: network technology that multiplexes multiple, independent network carriers on a single cable.

broadcast address: a media-specific or IP address referring to all stations on a media.

broadcasting: the act of sending to the broadcast address.

bps: bits per second.

bridge: a computer that connects two or more networks.

C

C: the "C" programming language.

Case Diagram: a pictorial representation of the relationship between counter objects in a MIB.

CCITT: *see International Telephone and Telegraph Consultative Committee.*

checksum: an arithmetic sum used to verify data integrity.

CL-mode: *see connectionless-mode network service.*

CLTS: connectionless-mode transport service.

CMIP: *see Common Management Information Protocol.*

CMIP over TCP: a mapping of the OSI network management framework to management of networks based on the Internet suite of protocols.

CMIS: Common Management Information Service.

CMISE: *see Common Management Information Service Element.*

CMOT: *see CMIP over TCP.*

CO-mode: *see connection-oriented mode.*

Common Management Information Protocol: the OSI protocol for network management.

Common Management Information Service: the service offered by CMIP.

Common Management Information Service Element: the application service element responsible for exchanging network management information.

community: an administrative relationship between SNMP entities.

community name: an opaque string of octets identifying a community.

community profile: that portion of the managed objects on an agent that a member of the community is allowed to manipulate.

connection-less mode: a service that does not provide a handshaking such as to guarantee delivery of data.

connection-oriented mode: a service that has handshaking such that data delivery is guaranteed.

CONS: connection-oriented network service.

COTS: connection-oriented transport service.

D

DARPA: *see Defense Advanced Research Projects Agency.*

DARPA Internet: *see Internet.*

data: the user information.

data link layer: that portion of an OSI system responsible for transmission, framing, and error control over control over a single communications link.

datagram: a self-contained unit of data transmitted independently of other datagrams.

default route: when sending an IP datagram, an entry in the routing table which will be used if no other route is appropriate.

default route: when sending an IP datagram, an entry in the routing table which will be used if no route is appropriate.

Defense Advanced Research Projects Agency: an agency of the U.S. Department of Defense that sponsors high-risk, high-payoff research. The Internet suite of protocols was developed under DARPA auspices. DARPA was previously known as ARPA, the Advanced Research Projects Agency, when the ARPANET was built.

device: a network element of some kind.

direct routing: the process of sending an IP datagram when the destination resides on the same IP network (or IP subnet) as the sender.

dotted quad notation: a convention for writing IP addresses in textual format.

E

EGP: *see Exterior Gateway Protocol.*

end-system: a network device performing functions from all layers of the OSI model. End-systems are commonly thought of as hosting applications.

End-System to Intermediate-System Protocol: the ISO protocol used for gateway detection and address resolution.

end-to-end services: the services collectively offered by the lower three layers of the OSI model.

ES: *see end-system.*

ES-IS: *see End-System to Intermediate-System Protocol.*

experimental MIB: a MIB module defined in the experimental portion of the Internet management space.

Exterior Gateway Protocol: a protocol used by gateways in a multinet network environment to determine that a piece of equipment can be reached.

External Data Representation: a transfer syntax defined by Sun Microsystems, Inc.

F

Federal Research Internet: *see Internet.*

File Transfer Protocol: the application protocol offering file service in the Internet suite of protocols.

FIN: the finish bit in a TCP segment.

flow control: the mechanism whereby a receiver informs a sender how much data it is willing to accept.

fragment: an IP datagram containing only a portion of the user-data from a larger IP datagram.

fragmentation: the process of breaking an IP datagram into smaller parts, such that each fragment can be transmitted in whole on a given physical medium.

frame: packet transmitted across a media.

FTP: *see File Transfer Protocol.*

G

gateway: a router connecting two or more networks.

GOSIP: Government Open Systems Interconnection Profile.

H

hardware address: *see media address.*

header: *see protocol control information.*

HEMS: *see High-level Entity Management System.*

High-level Entity Management System: an early internetwork management experiment.

host: an end-system.

host-identifier: that portion of an IP address corresponding to the host on the IP network.

host-number: that portion of a sub-networked IP address corresponding to the host-number on the subnet.

I

IAB: *see Internet Activities Board.*

IANA: *see Internet Assigned Numbers Authority.*

ICMP: *see Internet Control Message Protocol.*

IEEE: *see Institute of Electrical and Electronics Engineers.*

IESG: *see Internet Engineer Steering Group.*

IETF: *see Internet Engineering Task Force.*

indirect routing: the process of sending an IP datagram to a gateway for forwarding to the final destination.

instance: *see object instance.*

instance-identifier: a means of identifying an instance of a particular object type.

Institute of Electrical and Electronics Engineers: a professional organization, which as a part of its duties to the community, performs some pre-standardization work for OSI.

interface layer: the layer in the Internet suite of protocols responsible for transmission on a single physical network.

intermediate-system: a network device performing functions from the three lower-layers of the OSI model. Intermediate-systems are commonly thought of as routing data for end-systems.

International Organization for Standardization: the organization that produces many of the world's standards. OSI is only one of many areas standardized by the ISO/IEC.

International Telephone and Telegraph Consultative Committee: a body comprising the national Post, Telephone, and Telegraph (PTT) administrations.

Internet: a collection of connected networks, primarily in the United States, running the Internet suite of protocols. Sometimes referred to as the DARPA Internet, NSF/DARPA Internet, or the Federal Research Internet.

Internet Activities Board: the technical body overseeing the development of the Internet suite of protocols.

Internet Assigned Numbers Authority: the entity responsible for assigning numbers in the Internet suite of protocols.

Internet Community: anyone, anywhere, who uses the Internet suite of protocols.

Internet Control Message Protocol: a simple reporting protocol for IP networks.

Internet Drafts: a means of documenting the work in progress of the IETF.

Internet Engineering Steering Group: the group coordinating the activities of the IETF.

Internet Engineering Task Force: a task force of the Internet Activities Board charged with resolving the short-term needs of the Internet.

internet layer: the layer in the Internet suite of protocols responsible for providing transparency over both the topology of the internet and the transmission media used in each physical network.

Internet Protocol: the network protocol offering a connectionless-mode network service in the Internet suite of protocols.

Internet suite of protocols: a collection of computer-communications protocols, originally developed under DARPA sponsorship. The Internet suite of protocols is currently the de facto answer to open systems.

internet: a network—with the Internet being the largest internet in existence.

Internet—standards Network Management Framework: RFC's 1155, 1156, and 1157.

Internet-standard MIB: RFC 1156.

Internet-standard SMI: RFC 1155.

IP address: a 32-bit quantity used to represent a point of attachment to the internet.

ISO Development Environment: a research tool developed to study the upper-layers of OSI.

ISO/IEC: *see International Organization for Standardization.*

ISODE: *see ISO Development Environment.*

K

kernel dive: the process of reading information out of the kernel.

L

LAN: *see local area network.*

LAP/LAPB: modified form of HDLC used as link level protocol for X.25.

layer management entity: in OSI, the instrumentation within a layer which talks to the SMAE.

leaf object: an object type defined in a MIB module which has no child nodes. In particular, tables and rows are not leaf objects.

lexicographic ordering: an ordering methodology.

lightweight presentation protocol: a protocol implementing a minimal OSI presentation service, but doing so using a special-purpose protocol.

LME: *see layer management entity.*

local area network: any one of a number of technologies providing high speed, short delay, with limited geographical size.

LPP: *see lightweight presentation protocol.*

M

managed node: a network device containing a network management agent implementation.

management framework: *see Internet-standard Network Management.*

Management Information Base: a collection of objects that can be accessed via a network management protocol. See Structure of Management Information.

management protocol: *see network management protocol.*

management station: *see network management station.*

maximum transmission unit: the largest amount of user-data that can be sent in a single frame on a particular media.

media address: the address of the physical interface.

media device: a low-level device which does not use a protocol at the internet layer as its primary function.

MIB: *see Management Information Base.*

MIB Module: a collection of managed objects.

MIB view: *see view.*

MIB-I: *see the Internet-standard MIB.*

MIB-II: currently RFC 1158 and RFCs.

MTU: *see maximum transmission unit.*

multi-homed: a host or gateway with more than one attachment to an IP network.

N

National Bureau of Standards: *see National Institute of Standards and Technology.*

National Institute of Standards and Technology: the branch of the U.S. Department of Commerce charged with keeping track of standardization. Previously known as the National Bureau of Standards.

NBS: *see National Institute of Standards and Technology.*

network: a collection of sub-networks connected by intermediate-systems and populated by end-systems.

network byte order: the Internet-standard ordering of the bytes corresponding to numeric values.

network layer: that portion of an OSI system responsible for data transfer across the network, independent of both the media comprising the underlying sub-networks and the topology of those sub-networks.

network management: the technology used to manage an internet.

network management agent: the implementation of a network management protocol which exchanges network management information with a network management station.

network management protocol: the protocol used to convey management information.

network management station: the system responsible for managing a network.

network-identifier: that portion of an IP address corresponding to a network in an Internet.

NIST: *see National Institute of Standards and Technology.*

NMS: *see network management station.*

NSF: National Science Foundation.

NSF/DARPA Internet: *see Internet.*

O

OSI: *see Open Systems Interconnection.*

Open Systems Interconnection: an international effort to facilitate communications among computers of different manufacture and technology.

P

passive open: the sequence of events occurring when an application entity informs the TCP that it is willing to accept connections.

PDU: *see protocol data unit.*

PE: *see presentation element.*

physical layer: that portion of an OSI system responsible for the electromechanical interface to the communications media.

ping: a program used to used to test IP-level connectivity from one IP address to another.

port number: identifies an application entity to a transport service in the Internet suite of protocols.

presentation element: in the ISODE, a "C" data structure capable of representing any ASN.1 object in a machine independent form.

presentation stream: a set of routines providing an abstraction of elements.

protocol control information: a data object exchanged by machines. It usually contains protocol information as well as data.

protocol data unit: a data object exchanged by machines, containing both protocol and user data.

protocol machine: a finite state machine, that is used to implement a particular protocol.

prototype: object type corresponding to an instance.

PTT: the post, telephone, and telegraph authority.

R

reassembly: the process of recombining fragments, at the final destination, into the original protocol packet.

Request for Comments: the document series describing the Internet suite of protocols and related experiments.

RFC: *see Request for Comments.*

router: a piece of software or hardware that directs packets through a network.

RS232: a standard of EIA for serial communications.

S

segment: a unit of used in network exchanges.

selector: a portion of an address identifying a particular entity at an address.

service primitive: a method of modeling how a service is requested or accepted by a user.

session layer: that portion of an layered system responsible for adding control mechanisms to a data exchange.

SGMP: *see Simple Gateway Monitoring Protocol.*

Simple Gateway Monitoring Protocol: the predecessor of SNMP.

Simple Gateway Transfer Protocol: the application protocol offering message handling.

Simple Gateway Management Protocol: the application protocol offering network management in the Internet suite of Protocols.

SMAE: *see System Management Application-Entity.*

SMI: *see Structure of Management Information.*

SMTP: *see Simple Mail Transfer Protocol.*

SMUX: *see SNMP Multiplexing Protocol.*

SMUX peer: an application entity which has formed a SMUX association with an SNMP agent.

SNMP: *see Simple Network Management Protocol.*

SNMP Multiplexing Protocol: a local-mechanism used for communication between an SNMP agent and an arbitrary user-process.

SNMP Working Group: the working group of the IETF which standardized the technology used for network management.

SNPA: sub-network point of attachment.

socket: a pairing of an IP address and a port number.

Structure of Management Information: the rules used to define the objects that can be accessed via a network management protocol. see Management Information Base.

subnet: a physical network within an IP network.

subnet mask: a 32-bit quantity indicating which bits in an IP address that particular physical network within an IP network.

sub-network: a single network connecting several nodes on a single transmission media.

SYN: the synchronize bit in a TCP segment.

system management: the OSI name for network management.

system management application-entity: in an OSI system, the process responsible for coordinating between the LMEs and the management protocol.

T

TCP: *see Transmission Control Protocol.*

TCP/IP: *see Internet suite of protocols.*

TELNET: the application protocol offering virtual terminal service.

three-way handshake: a process whereby two protocol entities synchronize during connection establishment.

TLV: tag, length and value.

traceroute: a program used to determine the route taken by a packet across a network.

Transmission Control Protocol: a transport protocol offering a connection oriented transport service.

transport layer: that portion of a layered protocol responsible for reliability and multiplexing of data transfer across a network.

transport-stack: the combination of protocols, at the transport layer and below.

trivial authentication: password-based.

U

UDP: *see User Datagram Protocol.*

upper-layer protocol number: identifies a transport entity to the IP.

URG: the urgent bit in a TCP segment.

urgent data: user-data delivered in sequence but somehow more interesting to the receiving application entity.

User Datagram Protocol: the transport protocol offering a connectionless-mode transport service in the Internet suite of protocols.

user-data: conceptually, the part of a protocol data unit used to transparently communicate information between the users of the protocol.

V

variable: a pairing of an object instance name and associated value.

view: the collection of managed objects realized by an agent which is visible to a community.

W

WAN: *see wide area network.*

well-known port: a transport endpoint which is documented by the IANA.

wide area network: any one of a number of technologies providing geographically distant transfer.

X

X.121: the addressing format used by X.25 based networks.

X.25: a connection-oriented network facility.

X.409: the predecessor to Abstract Syntax Notation One.

XDR: *see External Data Representation.*

Y

yacc: yet another compiler compiler.

Acronyms

AARP—AppleTalk address resolution protocol

ACK—Acknowledgement

ACS—Asynchronous communication server

ACSE—association control service element

AIX—Advanced interactive executive (IBM's UNIX look a like)

ANSI—American National Standards Institute

ARE—All routes explorer

ARP—Address resolution protocol

ARPA—Advanced Research Project Agency

ARPANET—Advanced Research Project Agency Network

ARQ—Automatic Repeat Request

ASE—application-service element

ASN.1—Abstract Syntax Notation One

ATM—Asynchronous transfer mode

BBN—Bolt, Beranek and Newman

BER—basic encoding rules

BNF—Backus - Naur Form

bps—Bits per second

BSC—Binary synchronous communications

BSD—Berkley Software Distribution

BTU—Basic transmission unit

CCITT—International Consultative Committee on Telegraphy and Telephony

CLNP—Connectionless network protocol

CMIP—Common management information protocol

CMIS—Common management information service

CMISE—Common management information service element

CMIP—Common Management Information Protocol

CMIPDU—Common management information protocol data unit

CMOL—CMIP on IEEE 802.2 Logical Link Control

CMOT—Common management information protocol over TCP/IP

CMU—Carnegie-Mellon University

CRC—cyclic-redundancy check

CREN—The Corporation for Research and Educational Networking

DARPA—Defense Advanced Research Projects Agency

DCA—Defense Communication Agency

DCE—Data Communications Equipment

DDN—Defense data network

DDP—Datagram delivery Protocol

DES—data-encryption standard

DIX—Digital , Intel and Xerox

DLC—Data link control

DNS—Domain name server

DSU/CSU—Data service unit/channel service unit

DTE—Data Terminal Equipment

DTR—Data terminal ready

EBCDIC—Extended binary coded decimal interchange code

EGP—external gateway protocol

EIA—Electronic Industry Association

EMA—Enterprise management architecture

ES-IS—end system to intermediate system

FDDI—fiber-distributed data interface

FTP—file-transfer protocol

GOSIP—Government Open Systems Interconnection Profile

HEMS—high-level entity-management system

HDLC—high-level data-link control

HMP—host-monitoring protocol
IAB—Internet Activities Board
ICMP—internet-control message protocol
IEN—Internet Engineering Notes
IETF—Internet Engineering Task Force
IP—internet protocol
IS-IS—intermediate system to intermediate system
ISO—International Organization for Standardization
kbps—Kilo Bits Per Second
LAN—local area network
LLC—Logical link control
LMMS—LAN/MAN management services
LMMU—LAN/MAN management user
LMMPE—LAN/MAN management protocol entity
MAN—metropolitan area network
MD5—Message Digest 5
MIB—management information base
MIT—Massachusetts Institute of Technology
NME—network-management entity
NFS—Network File System
NSAP—network service-access point
NAK—Negative Acknowledgement
NSFNET—National Science Foundation Network
NOC—Network operations center
OO—Object-Oriented
OSI—Open systems interconnection
OSPF—Open shortest path first
PAD—Packet Assembler Disassembler
PDU—Protocol data unit
PING—Packet InterNet Groper
PPP—Point to Point Protocol
RFC—Request for comments
RIP—Routing Information Protocol
RMON—Remote network monitoring

ROSE—Remote-operations-service element

SAP—Service-access point

SDLC—Synchronous Data Link Control

SDU—Service data unit

SGMP—Simple gateway-monitoring protocol

SLIP—Serial Line/IP

SMAE—Systems-management application entity

SMAP—Systems-management application process

SMASE—Systems-management application-service element

SMF—Systems-management function

SMFA—Systems-management functional area

SMI—Structure of management information

SMP—Simple management protocol

SMTP—Simple mail-transfer protocol

SNA—System Network Architecture

SNMP—simple network-management protocol

SNMPv2—simple network-management protocol version 2

TCP—transmission-control protocol

UDP—user datagram protocol

WAN—wide area network

Index

802 model of network management, 26–27

A

ACCESS clause, 91
accounting management, 27
ACTIONS, 67
agents, 25, 26, 32, 34, 55, 56, 66, 149–53
    interface errors and, 105
    proxy, 131–33
    relationship of managers and, 30
agent vendors, 18–19
aggregate error, 123
American National Standards Institute, 18
ANS, 9
API (Application Programming Interface), 147
archival and retrieval of historic data, 31
ASN (Abstract Syntax Notation), 28
ASN.1 (Abstract Syntax Notation One), 64

terminology and notation, 65
ASN.1 compilers, 79

B

BEDLs (Basic Encoding and Decoding Library), 147
BER (Basic Encoding Rules), 64, 65–66
bilingual managers, 133–34
binding error, 123, 124
books and related writing on SNMP, 13–15
Bosco, Paul, 2, 3
B-Tree (balanced tree structure), 66–67

C

Case, J., 80
CERFNet, 9
Chapin, A. L., 14
CICnet, 9
CMIP (Common Management Information Protocol), 22, 52
    model, 25–27